Audible Adventures Presents:

A Guide for Time-Travelers
visiting the estate owned by The Beatles' George Harrison

Written & Designed by THE CARDINALS

Welcome to Friar Park
A Guide for Time-Travelers visiting the estate
owned by The Beatles' George Harrison. Vol. I

Copyright 2019
by Scott Cardinal

All Rights Reserved. No part of this publication may be reproduced, stored in a retrieval system, or transmitted in any form or by any means, electronic, email, photocopying, recording, scanning, or otherwise, without the prior written permission of the Publisher. The content of this book is of a historical, educational, and newsworthy nature, and is made available in the name of the public interest. Considering the purpose and character of the transformative use of the text and photos in creating a new work, the Publisher is confident that their use does not directly affect and/ or compete with any potential claimant's business or potential for income. The Publishers are confident that there is no part of this book that is in violation of, or infringes upon, anyone's copyrights, trademarks, licensing, privacy, or postmortem publicity rights.

Limit of Liability/Disclaimer of Warranty: While the Publishers and the Author(s) have used their best efforts in preparing this book, they make no representations or warranties with respect to the accuracy or completeness of the contents of this book and specifically disclaim any implied warranties of merchantability or fitness for a particular purpose. Neither the Publisher nor the Author(s) shall be liable for any loss of profit or any other commercial damages, including, but not limited to, special, incidental, consequential, or other damages.

All reasonable effort has been made to contact the photographers and copyright owners of all images printed in this publication. Any omissions or errors are inadvertent and will be corrected in subsequent editions, provided written notification is sent to the Publisher. Many of the images in this book are transformative works and are protected by their own copyrights as well as the overall copyright protecting the contents of this book.

For information on books published by the Campfire Network, or for bulk & wholesale orders, or to schedule interviews with the Author, please contact Cardinal@CampfireNetwork.com. Please visit AudibleAdventures.com

Disclaimer: "Ye Friends of Friar Park" is neither associated with, nor endorsed by, The Beatles, Apple Corps Limited, or the Estate of George Harrison.

Special thanks to my friends Gerhard Bohrer and Servi Stevens for sharing their collections and providing enthusiasm & encouragement.

Audible Adventures Presents:

Preface

Friar Park is one of England's most extraordinary country homes. Located in the charming town of Henley-on-Thames, it is quite unlike anything most people have ever seen before. In addition to its extraordinary mansion, there are also enchanting lodges along and within the perimeter, and what remains of a "museum of gardens" that had included an astonishing variety of botanical wonders that were a feast for the eyes of all visitors. As of the date of publications, Friar Park is only accessible to those personally invited by the family of musician George Harrison. However, between the years 1895-1919, when it was the home of Sir Frank and Lady Crisp and their children, a vast number of visitors were welcome on certain days of certain months of the year, in order for them to enjoy strolling through its gardens.

Upon arriving at the property, visitors were offered the opportunity to purchase the latest edition of the GUIDE FOR THE USE OF

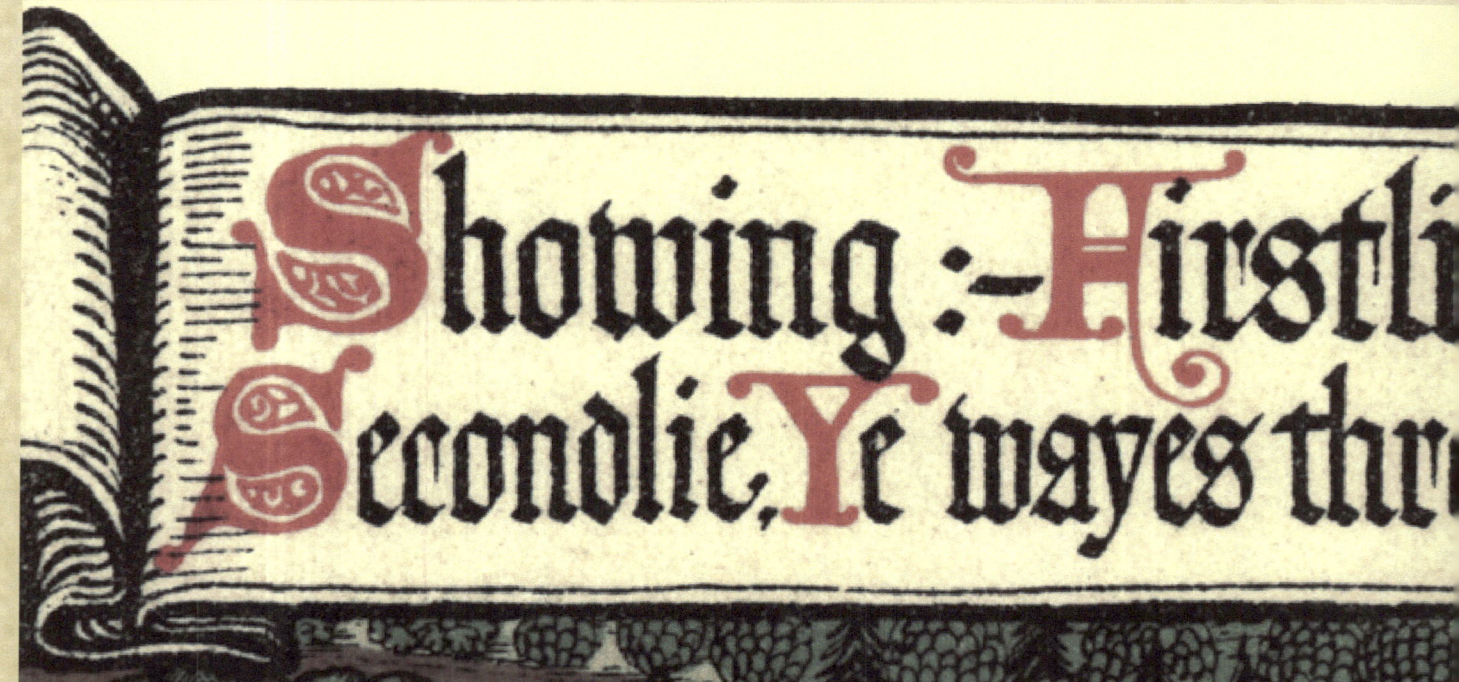

VISITORS TO FRIAR PARK written by Frank Crisp himself.

Though the Guide did offer plenty of useful tips to properly navigate through the grounds and gardens, readers may have felt that they were being subjected to a rather tedious dissertation that was filled to the brim with esoteric information that was of little interest to them.

Truth be told, even I had a tough time getting though it! As a consequence, I imagined what might manifest if I could travel back in time to met with Frank Crisp and offer to put together a different type of "guide for visitors" that might have a wider appeal.

It would be utterly presumptuous of me to assume that this guide in your hands is the sort that should instead have been offered to visitors to Friar Park in the early days of the 20th century, but I am indeed quite confident that this is the sort of guide that should be made available for anyone with any interest in knowing what it was like to visit Friar Park when Friar Park was newly built and astonishing visitors from around the world.

Take note, Friar Park today is a far cry from Friar Park 100 years ago. Given a chance to visit Friar Park at this time, I highly recommend you do so. But given a choice between visiting today or visiting in 1919 via time-travel, I highly recommend you choose the latter.

So wherever - and whenever - you may be when reading these words - whether at the gates of Friar Park, or walking along one of the many paths of the estate, or if you are in the comfort of your own home, or anywhere else where you can sit in peace and quiet, with a cup of coffee or tea, or perhaps if you have indeed traveled-back in time and have found yourself at the grand estate, kindly prepare yourself for an incredible adventure!

We bid you welcome to Friar Park.

Dedication:

This book is dedicated to the genius Sir Frank Crisp.
If not for him, there would have been no Friar Park,
and you would not be reading this.

In loving memory of:
Jasper, who sat by my side for 14 years.

He brought love and joy to our hearts and home, and
though he took so much when he left for Kittyland, a
treasure-trove has been left behind that
we will cherish for the rest of our days,
until we see him again.

Preface
Prepare for ye time-travel adventure!

Journey to Friar Park
From London by train to Marlow and then steamship to Henley-on-Thames and sauntering through the town to the estate.

Meet Sir Frank Crisp
Ye Lord & Ideator of Friar Park.

Entrance to Friar Park
Ornate Gates, Pillars, and Designs.

Ye Lower Lodge
Built for the estate manager & head gardener Mr. Philip Knowles.

Road to Ye Friar's Abode
Take a horse-drawn carriage or walk to the grand mansion built by Frank Crisp.

Meet Mr. Knowles
Gallant Gardener of ye grand estate.

Don't Keep off the Grass
Ye verily puzzling sign that greets all visitors.

Ye Gloomie Glenne
Descend down quaggy, leaf-carpeted path 'tween exposed tree roots.

Ye Small Byrdies Paradise
Hearken & see feathered friends in the branches and sky above.

Ye Alpine Meadow
Flowers hence here, there, and otherwhere!

Ye Stone of Precation
Judge not what you dislike, but appreciate what is for thy pleasure.

Ye Waye throughe ye Woode
Where wildlife enjoy shade and seeds.

Ye Place for Ye Calme Reflexion
Whereat warm water flows & breezes blow by and the trees gently sway.

Ye Water Lilies
Thither toward colorful floating jewels.

Ye Sham-Rock Garden & Tea House
'Tis real rocks or not? Explore for yourself.

Ye Middle Lodge
Where methinks ye guests may stay in comfort.

Ye Long Walke of Coole & Shade
Shady path through canopy of mature trees.

Where ye Echo Lays
'Tis an astonishing approach.

Ye Friar's Abode
Facade & entry of the manor with crinkum-crankum where Lord & Lady may be found.

Ye Terrace Garden & Ye Fountain of Perpetual Mirth
Dutch knots, both geometrical & symmetrical.

Ye Pathe of Joye
For traversing north or south across lawn.

Ye Stepping Stones
Wander yonder water, confound & affright!

Ye Japanese Garden
Seek serenity in this Zen sanctuary.

Ye North & South Pooles
Demesne of freshwater species & illusions.

Ye Stone Brydge
Whither betwixt goodlie pooles.

Ye Water Caves
Wondrous mystery & magic await thee as ye row underground!

Ye Treasured Memories
Leave nothing but footprints, take nothing but memories.

Journey to Friar Park from London

There comes upon you the year 1899. You are in London. A strong breeze blows to your right as you ascend into your horse-drawn carriage which begins heading toward Paddington Station. As you know, in the late 19th century London is the largest city in the world. It is an exciting place to be and it is an exciting time to be here. There are so many life-changing technological inventions. Many of which make life a lot easier for everybody. Well, almost everybody. This place smells pretty bad. The streets are filled with sewage, and horse manure, and most people have never had a bath in their entire lives. There is a lot of smoke in the air. The coal fires produces a horrible smog. Because most people don't have indoor plumbing they throw buckets filled with body waste out of their windows and into the streets. It's really gross. Of course, the city has come a long way since the days of what was called The Great Stink. That was an event in central London - just 40 years ago - in the summer of 1858. As it turned out, the miserably hot weather exacerbated the smell of untreated human waste that had accumulated along the banks of the River Thames. So, yes, life is absolutely miserable for many. But life is not miserable for everybody. There are plenty of shopkeepers and merchants who do not live in poverty. And obviously the wealthiest citizens live luxuriously in beautiful mansions furnished with antiques and the finest of everything. And some even have country homes outside of London, in places such as Henley-on-Thames. And that is the location of your destination today.

Your horse-drawn carriage drops you off in front of Paddington Station. This site has been the London terminus of the Great Western Railway since 1838. During the early part of this century, British life changed quite a bit due to the introduction of, and expansion of, the railway system. Before trains were around, the British traveled by foot or horse or in carriages while on land. They also made use of the assortment of canals, that they traveled upon in boats of various sizes. Though steam locomotives began being used in 1804, it wasn't until 1833 that they started carrying human passengers. Throughout the rest of the 19th century, rail travel has became more and more popular. It was also a lot cheaper and quicker than coach travel. But even though thousands of miles of track have been laid down, sometimes in order to reach certain destinations people combined walking, carriages, trains, and steamships.

Such is the case when traveling from London to Henley-on-Thames. You will be traveling comfortably in a luxurious saloon carriage to convey your party to Marlow. Marlow is 31.2 miles from Paddington Station. It will take about an hour to get there.

You spend the majority of the trip speaking with other members of the Horticultural Club; many of whom you have known for many years. Though not all have extraordinary gardens, most do have very beautiful gardens. And nearly everyone is very knowledgable about various aspects of horticulture.

When you arrive in Marlow you proceed on foot through the pretty and quaint village toward the river-side. Marlow is located on the River Thames, where the road from Reading to High Wycombe crosses the river. In Old English, the town's name means, "Land after the draining of a pond". By the year 1227 it had its own market. There has been a bridge over the Thames at Marlow since the reign of King Edward III in the 1300s. From 1301 to 1307 the town had its own member of Parliament.

Below illustration shows what London looked like in the 1800s.

Journey to Friar Park from London

Marlow is one of the pleasantest river centers I know of. It is a bustling, lively little town; not very picturesque on the whole, it is true, but there are many quaint nooks and corners to be found in it, nevertheless. (Three Men in a Boat, 1889)

As you walk along the antiquated streets you are entranced by the many charming houses - many from the 15th though the 18th century. There are even some houses in the area from the 14th century. You walk down the long avenue called High Street and pass the "George and Dragon." Parallel to this is St. Peter Street. It used to be called "Duck Lane" due to the historical ducking chair that was once set on the banks of the river during the Middle Ages and served to punish the disgraced and criminals. The victims were tied to the chair and submerged in water using a special mechanism, similar to a swing. There is evidence that the same chair was used for ducking those who were accused of being witches.

You soon come across All Saints Church on the shore of the river near Marlow Bridge. It was erected in 1835 on the site of an earlier church and the spire contains eight bells. You continue your walk toward the historic bridge. There has been a bridge across the Thames at Marlow since before 1227. When you reach the river bank you enjoy a beautiful view of Marlow Lock and a hotel that was built in 1658. Once you arrive at the river-side you see your host, Mr. Frank Crisp. He welcomes you aboard a handsome steam launch.

As the vessel you are on glides against the swift current, you take in the view of the charming panorama of wooded hills, interspersed here and there with beautiful mansions. To your left is the Bisham Abbey that was built around 1260. You then pass the 18th century Georgian Manor house known as the Harleyford Estate. It is considered to be one of the most beautiful private country estates in the South of England. Parts of the grounds are attributed to the 18th Century landscape designer Capability Brown. You then pass The Olde Bell hotel which was founded in 1135, making it one of the oldest hotels in the world.

Your voyage continues as the steamer passes the Hambleden Lock and you see the beautiful Hambleden Water Mill across the river. After the lock, you can see the large white mansion, known as Greenlands across the river. Sailing forward against a swift current you see Temple Island. On it is an ornamental folly that was designed and constructed in 1771 as a fishing lodge. To your right is the beautiful country house known as Fawley Court. To your left is the Leander Club, which was founded in 1818, and is one of the oldest rowing clubs in the world.

You have finally reached Henley-on-Thames. It is located 35 miles west of London, and 23 miles from Oxford. This is a beautiful medieval town that is situated on the north bank of the winding River Thames in Oxfordshire. In the distance you see the Henley Bridge. The earliest recording of a bridge in this location dates back to the year 1232. The one today is a road bridge built in 1786. The bridge has five elliptical stone arches, and links Hart Street in Henley with White Hill leading up a steep hill to Remenham Hill. In the book The Henley Guide, written in 1826, Henley is described as follows:

HENLEY-UPON-THAMES is a clean and cheerful town, situated near the base of a cluster of hills, in one of the most agreeable windings of the River Thames. The Inns are numerous and afford excellent accommodation to parties visiting the town for the amusement of angling, the salubrity of its air, or the beauty of its scenery.

Comfortable lodgings may also be procured in the town or neighborhood. For centuries wealthy families have owned Country Houses in Henley so they could live in beautiful surroundings while also having easy access to London. And that is what brings you here right now. To your right are a series of Boat Houses along the waterside. One of which belongs to your host, Mr. Frank Crisp. It is located on WHARF LANE. This elegant property was built in 1892 as the party and boat house to Friar Park. Its location is perfect for watching the Royal Regatta! In fact, it is right opposite the famous Regatta finishing line. The building is beautiful, with its white stucco and exposed wood facing the water. The sides have red bricks rising two stories high. To the south is a gable with a gargoyle on its peak. On the north is an octagonal-shaped gable with an ornate weather-vane atop. Along the balcony are painted balustrades. Below is a boat launch on the left and glass doors leading to the dock to the right. On the north side is an additional lot with a garden and what seems to be a sort of rock grotto. It is here where Frank Crisp would entertain visitors, and sometimes provide lunch and tea, before personally accompanying them to his house and gardens. It must have been quite an experience to be seated upon its upstairs balcony, with the cool breezing coming in from along the Thames, while watching the boats go by, in the late 1800s, and anytime since then. It has a 45 ft. by 9 ft. Wet Dock.

Once inside you and your party are led upstairs to a room that can easily accommodate 80 people. The Dining Room leads on to a balcony which overlooks the river and beautiful scenery opposite. Sir Frank and Lady Crisp and their spectacular staff have clearly anticipated everything perfectly. Lunch is already waiting for you and your party. It has been quite a journey so far, and the day has barely begun. So sit down. Enjoy your lunch, and drink some tea.

Once done it will be time to journey to Friar Park.

Journey through Henley-on-Thames to Friar Park

You are standing along the private street that runs in front of Frank Crisp's boathouse. From the riverside it will take about 15 minutes to walk through the town of Henley to Friar Park. Someone in the party mentioned that it will be 2,700 feet total from here. At that point, many of the ladies and gentlemen decide to be conveyed to Friar Park aboard one of the carriages that Frank Crisp provided. It is such a lovely day outside that walking seems to be the best option, so you decide to do that. Some members of the Horticulture Club have walked through this storybook town before, and have said that there are many wonderful things to see, such as the historic church, the comfortable inns, the numerous bakeries and breweries, dozens of local shops selling items that people want and need, and the charming architecture and countless delightful buildings.

It was less than a decade ago when the 1891 edition of The Kelly's Directory described Henley-on-Thames as, **"The Pretties summer retreat in the county, surrounded by handsome villas and plantations, a very favorite and fashionable place to resort."**

You begin by traveling south on Wharf Lane and then along Thameside, the road that runs along the river. There are attractive buildings to your right, some with brick, and others with stucco facades, with grand views of the river to your left. After one block you reach an intersection. If you turn left, you will be on White Hill, which will bring you on to the Henley Bridge. This point of the Thames has been used for crossing since ancient times. Turning right, the road is Hart Street, which leads to the heart of Henley. The RED LION INN is located on the corner, to your right. You walk alongside of it, along the driveway where carriages can pull in and turn around. This coaching hotel named the Red

Lion has stood on this site, by the river at the foot of the bridge, for many centuries, and commands an amazing view of the river. King Charles I is known to have stayed here in 1632. It was here that 18th century poet William Shenstone wrote with a diamond on a pane of glass the following pleasing poem:

> To thee, fair Freedom! I retire
> From flatt'ry, cards, and dice, and din;
> Nor art thou found in mansions higher
> Than the low cot or humble Inn.
> 'Tis here with boundless pow'r I reign,
> And ev'ry health which I begin
> Converts dull port to bright Champaigne;
> Such freedom crowns it at an Inn.
>
> I fly from pomp, I fly from plate!
> I fly from Falsehood's specious grin!
> Freedom I love, and form I hate,
> And choose my lodgings at an Inn.
> Here, Waiter! take my sordid ore,
> Which lackies else might hope to win ;
> It buys what courts have not in store,
> It buys me freedom at an Inn.
> Whoever has travelled life's dull round;
> Wherever his stages may have been;
> May sigh to think he still has found.
> His warmest welcome at an inn.

Below: The view toward the Thames from the town of Henley.

Journey through Henley-on-Thames

You are now on Hart Street, which is Henley's oldest street. In 1826, the Henley Guide wrote the following: **Henley contains the following streets: Hart Street, High Street, West Street, Bell Street, New Street, Duke Street, and Friday Street. A plain stone cross stands at the intersection of the four principal streets. In the year 1781, an act was passed for building a new bridge and making commodious avenues thereto, widening the High Street and Market Place, and also for lighting, watching, and paving the streets of the town. They are now generally wide, well paved, and lighted, and though far from regular, the buildings are handsome and capacious; and the prosperity of the town is evinced by the improvements progressively taking place in the habitations of tradesmen of every rank.**

On your right is the ancient Parish Church of Saint Mary the Virgin. It is the entrance to the town itself. Some suspect that it may date back as far as 1,000 a.d., but it is known that it certainly does date back to at least the year 1204, with alterations and remodeling being done from the 15th through the 19th Centuries. It is certainly a handsome Gothic structure with its wide arched windows on the ground floor, and a tall tower on the west side, composed of intermingled flint and stone. The tower has battlements, and on each corner are octagonal turrets. Once you pass the church there are numerous buildings on your right and left, none more than three stories high, many of which have exposed beams with white stucco, in the Tudor style. Many have red or grey brick facades. Their red clay roofs and brick chimneys stand out against the bright blue sky above.

On your left is a two-story, 16th century, timber-framed building, with a facade that has been plastered over. It has a very large, steeply pitched, old tiled roof. There are two dormer windows in the attic. On the left side is a carriageway entrance beneath a load-bearing beam. Above that is an adorable little window, framed in wood.

Next to that is another two-story, 16th century building. 22 Hart Street is an old timber framed house that has plastered infill between exposed timbers. It also has an old roof of red clay tiles. On the same side, at 20 Hart Street, is an 18th century, two-story, timber-framed building. The facade is of grey brick with red brick window dressings. The top floor has three casement windows, and there is a steeply pitched tiled roof. There is a store front on the ground floor. At 18 Hart Street there is a three-story building with an 18th century facade. It has silver grey brick walls with red corner angles and window surrounds. It has a hipped, old tiled, roof. There is an adjoining two-story stable entrance, with a projecting first floor canted bay window. The east side of the facade has a large lantern projecting out of it. Next to that is a brick building, painted white, three-stories in height, with a bay window above the store front window. On the west side is a narrow carriageway that leads to a courtyard within. It is owned by the McBEAN BROTHERS. Among other things, they are Metal Workers, Coppersmiths, and

Electrical Bell Hangers. In their store they sell compact ladders, lawn mowers, knife machines, and mincers. They also sell cutlery, razors, and scissors. It's also a good place to get China and glasses. About 300 feet from the church, on your right, you see the WHITE HART INN. It has been here so long that it is said the street is named after it. There is a carriage entry on the left side of the buildings and a brick facade on the right, with a door and a bay window with leaded panes. Above it are four thin, tall windows with transoms. It has two gables and clay tiles on the roof. The earliest part of this building dates back to around the year 1300. It was extended to the rear in the early 1500s. Once one passes through the carriageway they will find themselves in a courtyard, surrounded by three ranges of buildings. They currently contain twenty guest chambers.

Keep walking and on your right you will see the Catherine Wheel Inn. It is three-stories high, with a brick facade, and hipped, tiled roof. There are six windows across the top floors. A pub has been at this location for more than 400 years. What has made this Inn so popular, along with its prime location on Hart Street, is that it has attached stables around the back. It is a popular place for Luncheons, Dinners, Teas, Wedding Breakfasts, and Banquets. They also have Billiard tables. It has always been one of the public coaching stops. Today, an Omnibus and Carriage currently stops in front of it to take guests back and forth to the trains. This inn is named after St. Catherine of Alexandria – a Christian Saint who was condemned to death on a spiked breaking wheel that shattered when she touched it. So, since they did not have another spiked breaking wheel handy, or they were afraid she would break that one, too, they just beheaded her.

You then reach the main crossroads. If you turn left, the road is Duke Street. It was formally known as Bridge Street because a small bridge used to span over the stream that once ran alongside of it. The name was then changed to Duck Street, and was then named Brook Street, but was later renamed Duke street. This street was considerably narrower thirty years ago, but it was widened in the years 1872 and 1873 by demolishing the buildings on its west side. The three-story building on the left has a rounded corner, with a bay window on the second floor, and has beautiful brickwork, combining dark bricks, with red brick around the dressings and windows. Across the street from that, also on your left, on the corner of Duke Street and Market Street is a three-story building that is occupied by a sugar confectioner. The building is not square-shaped. The wall and windows are instead arranged on an angle in order to take in a fine view of Hart Street.

In the center of the junction is a large, ornate, stone, drinking fountain. It has been in this spot since 1885, when it replaced an obelisk that was erected there in 1785, and recently had two lanterns on the south and north sides. The fountain is made of polished pink granite and limestone, designed in a gothic style, gabled with crockets and pinnacles, and is surmounted by a stone cross. There are plaques on each side, along with drinking fountain bowls. There are even dog bowls at the base. It has been placed here in memory of Reverend Greville Phillimore – a former rector. It is placed upon double stone slabs and is surrounded by four lamps with clear round globes. It is well-placed in the middle, and helps

Journey through Henley-on-Thames

Above: Illustration of the Thames during Henley's Royal Regatta

guide people as to which side they should travel on. As you stand here, a horse is pulling a wagon of wood, and along the sidewalk some men ride by on bicycles. Across the street you can see women pushing children in carriages.

If you turn right the road becomes Bell Street. It was formally known as North Street, but was renamed after the Bell Inn. From here you can see some of the businesses on Bell Street, including those dedicated to selling stationary, and other such items for ladies and gentleman, there is a store there that only sells hats, another sells only tailor-made suits. Over there is the substantial, stone-faced shop that belongs to a watchmaker and jeweler, and over there is a shop belonging to a draper.

If you were to turn right and then walk for roughly 585 ft., the Bull Inn will be on your left side. It was originally built in the 15th century. The building is mainly timber framed with a plaster infill on the top floor, with a tile roof and red brick chimney. It has three-bay windows with small gables atop. In the late seventeenth century, the structure was altered quite a bit. Directly to your right is a three-story building with a rounded brown brick facade. Canopies extend out into the street, over the sidewalks. In fact, you are standing beneath one of the canopies right now. Step out into the street and you will see that above the top floor windows are large letters that spell out the word CHEMISTS. This building will be lowered in height in the 20th century, which seems like a particularly unusual thing to do.

After crossing the junction you are now on Market Place, which opens out into a large, wedge-shaped area. Like Hart Street behind you, Market Street is filled with charming buildings with tudor style or red brick facades, or red-brick infill. Most buildings have hipped or pitched roofs covered in old clay tiles. Over there is a GROCER. They have an advertisement in the window that they sell fragrant lavender water. They also sell Rose, Orange, and Elder Flower Water. A few people are walking out right now after having purchased Schweppes soda water and lemonade. They also sell Otto of Rose cold cream, that its advertisement says is for *chapped hands, removing sunburns, and freckles, and that will render skin beautiful, soft, smooth and fair.* If you stroll in there you may also purchase white or brown Windsor soap, aromatic pastilles, and smelling salts. Oh, they also sell tooth and nail brushes. The second building on your right is the Feathers Hotel. It has a red brick facade, is three-stories high, and has three windows on the above floor. The door is directly in the center with a window in each side.

The third building on your right, at #6-8 Market Place, is the Oxford Temperance Hotel. It was established in 1882 by the Henley Coffee Tavern. It is three-stories in height, with a red brick facade, and red tile roof. The top floor is actually the attic, above yellow stone crown molding. It is open from 5:30 am to 11 pm. Hot dinners are served at midday on strict temperance principles. There are two multi-pane windows on each side of the door and three narrow rectangular windows along the second floor. In the center is a stone crest. It is not a large hotel. It only has five guest bedrooms. The hotel offers stabling for four horses. The entry is through two double wooden doors with a glass transom at the top.

In case you are wondering, the Total Abstinence Society, was formed in 1859 and met at the Old Assembly Rooms in Bell Street. I am not sure what the guest were abstaining from, but hopeful it was not liquor, since the small town is dotted with pubs and breweries. Next to the hotel is a three-story building with a red brick facade on the upper stories. There are two shallow canted oriel bay windows on the second floor. On the ground floor are double doors between shop front windows filled with goods for sale.

After walking about 150 ft. from the intersection behind you, look on your left and you will see that there is a three-story building referred to as The Argyle. There have been different businesses here for hundreds of years. Originally it was called The Cannon. It was then called The Hop Leaf. It was named The Argyll Hotel in 1887. There is an entry on the left hand side that leads into a carriage entry, with lanterns on the brick-lined walls. In twenty years it will be altered in a mock-Tudor fashion. On the ground floor are double-height casement windows. Above them, the top floors have decorative, Tudor-style moldings filled with stucco. On the right side of the building are sets of tracery casement windows that, at this time of day, are wide open, and

Journey through Henley-on-Thames

letting the breeze flow into the rooms. At the peak of the right side of the building is a gabled roof with ornate boards along the eaves for structural support, and are also decorative. But as it stands now, in 1899, The Argyll, along with the buildings to the right and left of it, have unadorned, red brick facades.

Built in 1749, the three-story building next door to the right at 17 Market Place, has a red brick facade with silver grey panels between windows. It has a moulded wood cornice and a tiled hipped roof. A few buildings up, on the same side, is 23 Market Place. It is an early 18th century, red and grey brick building, two-stories in height, with an old tile roof with two flat topped dormers. There is a door and a shop-front window on the ground floor. And over there, adjoining the Town Hall, is the Greyhound Hotel. It has a pub that offers cuisine wines and all sorts of spirits of the finest quality. On your left, the second building from the corner of the road, there is a clothing store that was opened in 1896 by brothers, Samuel, Thomas and John Facy. It is three-stories high, with a red stone facade. On your right is a two-story Tudor-style building with exposed vertical beams and two stained glass windows on the top floor and two stained glass bay windows on the second floor, topped with red clay tiles.

As of this date, 1899, the new Town Hall is not yet completed. It has been under construction since 1897 in the location of the previous Town Hall, and where there was a Market House in the late 1700s. The new building under construction was designed in a Palladian classical style, with red brick, and a colonnaded front. It is located right in the center of the street. Along the east facade is a rich display of Baroque ornament and plasterwork, with a grand pedimented front. There are two very narrow windows in each side and an ornate, round-headed window, between two rectangular windows on the top floor. They seem to be adding a tower on the top, likely as a look-out, but also for a clock that people can see from below. Once completed, there will be a wide space inside for selling grain, poultry, vegetables, and other items. Your group walks along the left side of the Town Hall, and continues walking westward, as the road continued its incline. From this vantage point, you see that the Town Hall is much longer than expected, with nine wide multi-paned windows on three separate floors, along with five dormer windows in the attic. Behind the Town Hall there is an option of turning right on Kings Road, which you do not do.

On your left is the Broad Gates Inn. It is located inside a former merchant's house that was built in the early 1500s. It became an inn in the 17th century. The ground floor has windows in either side of the carriage entry in the center. The top floor juts out over the ground floor and has wide windows in either side, and a smaller window over the carriage entry. The roof is covered in dark clay tiles.

The building next to that is the Cannon Inn. It is easy to spot since its sign projects out from the building and has an actual cannon on top of it.

You keep walking straight.

On the left hand side is a small chapel that was built in 1873, with a high-pitched gable and gothic-style windows. The facade is covered in grey brick, with red brick trimmings.

There are numerous two-story residential structures on your right, stepping up the hillside, as the road continues to ascend. They have all been built in the 19th century and have slate roofs.

At this point the name of the road becomes **GRAVEL HILL**. Gravel Hill predates the town itself, and there are references to it as far back as the 14th century. In fact, some houses around you were even built in the early 15th century. As Gravel Hill begins to slightly bend to the right you see, at 43 Gravel Hill, the Old Basketmaker's Arms. It has a white stucco facade and clay tile roof, with a wide chimney stack. The original building was built in about 1600, and was a pub for as long as anyone could remember.

Continue forward, and moments later the road suddenly widens. To the right is a road called **HOP GARDENS**. You can turn on to it, and then immediately turn right again. That road will be West Street, and head back down into town, parallel to Gravel Hill. But your group is walking straight up a wide driveway across the intersection. Stop and look both ways. Make sure no horse-drawn carriages are coming along. Okay, the coast is clear. Follow them. It sure looks like wonderful things await you up ahead. In fact, it looks as if you have finally arrived at the entry to Friar Park.

Below: Vintage postcard showing assorted images taken in the town of Henley and two photos taken at Friar Park.

Meet Frank Crisp

Unfortunately, not much is known of Lady Crisp, but here is what is known of Sir Frank's life: Frank Crisp was born in London on October 26th, 1843. His father was a successful printer. When Frank turned 16 he decided on a career as a lawyer. In 1867, when Frank was 23, he married Catherine Howes. In 1869 he passed the Law Society examination with honors, and qualified as a solicitor and began working in the area of commercial contracts for the firm of Ashurst & Morris. Among his clients were numerous foreign railroad companies and the Imperial Japanese Navy when their battleships were constructed in England. He eventually became a senior partner and the legal firm's name was changed to Ashurst, Morris, Crisp and Co., with offices at 17 Throgmorton Avenue. Among his responsibilities at the firm were drawing up the contracts for the cutting of the Cullinan diamond. As many people know, the Cullinan diamond was found on January 26th 1905 in a mine in South Africa. It is the largest gem-quality diamond ever found. It was originally over 3,100 carats and weighed 1.37 lb. His contribution to the firm was of such value that by 1888, he was receiving 25% of the firm's profits. By 1892, Frank Crisp was receiving 50% of the firm's profits. He had an unusual schedule. He arrived at the office from his home in Holland Park at 9:45 a.m. and worked throughout the day. For lunch, he typically only had a bar of chocolate. At 4:00 p.m. he took a brief break for toast and tea. He then continued working until 6:45 p.m. He would then leave for dinner and then return to the office at 8:00 p.m., where he would work until 10:00 p.m. He was knighted in 1907 and was created a Baronet in 1913. From that point forward, he was known as Sir Frank Crisp.

Above: Frank Crisp looking rather dapper while posing in his library.

This was an incredibly interesting man, with many interests, some of which included: horticulture, gardening, and natural history. When not at his home or office in London, he spent much of his personal time in Henley, where he actively participated in town affairs. Crisp also supported (and perhaps influenced the designs for) the new Congregationalist church, circa 1907. For his work in connection with horticultural science - and practice - he was awarded the Victoria Medal of Honor in Horticulture by the Royal Horticultural Society. Frank Crisp was the owner of one of the largest collections of microscopes in the world. He had been the President of the Horticultural Club, Vice-President and Treasurer of the Linnean Society of London, and Honorary Secretary of the Royal Microscopical Society.

Here is what is known of Frank Crisp's death, and following: Sir Frank Crisp died on April 29th, 1919. He was 75 years old. The funeral took place at Henley-on Thames, and it was evident from the aspect of the town that the inhabitants had lost a worthy citizen and one they held in high esteem and honor. His will had not been altered since 1871. It was made on a sheet of paper that contained less than 100 words. He bequeathed everything to his wife. There was no executor appointed. His eldest son, Frank Morris Crisp inherited his father's baronetcy. At the time of his death, Crisp's estate was valued for probate at nearly £7,000,000. With the family not having the means to maintain the large property, and perhaps not even having the interest to do so, they put Friar Park up for sale. The auction included the sale of the House, the Lodges, all 62 acres, and other houses that Crisp owned, including his large boat house on the river. The ESTATE AUCTION FLYER had the following information printed upon it:

Meet Frank Crisp

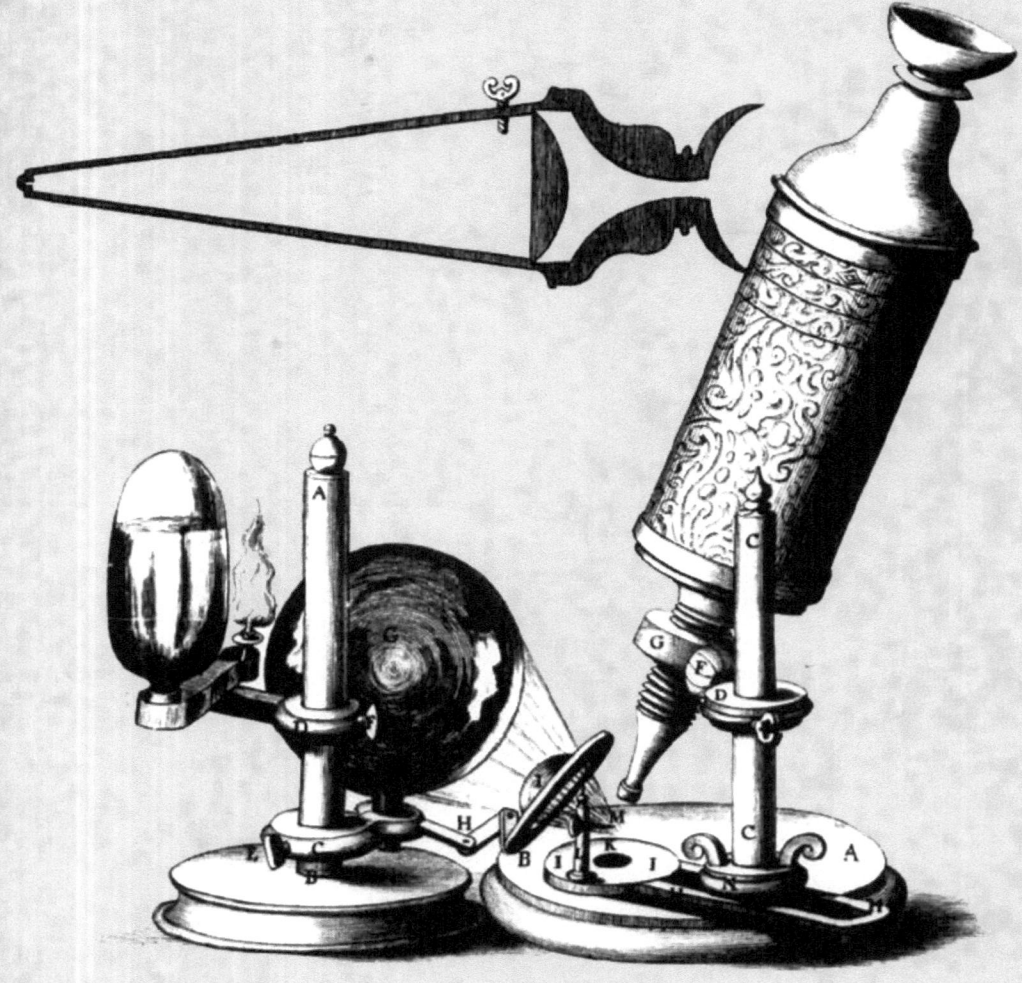

The Friar Park Estate,
Henley-on-Thames,
including **FRIAR PARK**,
(the seat of the late Sir Frank Crisp, Bart.,) with its
Exceptional Grounds & World-Famous Rock Garden,
comprising together 62 acres.

The elaborately designed and substantially built Country Residence magnificently placed on a peak of the Chilterns high above the Ancient Borough of Henley-on-Thames, within a mile of the Station, whence London is reached in an hour, and known as FRIAR PARK.

So, that is a glimpse into the interesting & honorable life of Sir Frank Crisp. He was the man who envisioned Friar Park, and financed Friar Park, and who built Friar Park, with the generous assistance of other accomplished geniuses at the time.

Ye Gate of Entrance for Ye Visitors

Downtown Henley and Thames River is that way.

W elcome to Friar Park. The year is 1899 and you have just arrived at the south entry gates to the grand estate.

The month is May. A balmy breeze blows in from the west as you feel the glowing rays of sunshine as they land upon your head and shoulders. You are standing on the edge of the broad driveway that leads into Friar Park. The gates are just under 100 ft. in front of you. On the right hand corner is a red-brick wall that was designed to look like a mini-watch tower. There are three deep-set stone arched windows along the exterior of the tower, and three facing within the gardens. Alongside of it is a low brick wall that is surmounted by an iron fence. There are trimmed evergreen hedges on the other side. The driveway leads to four tall gate piers. They are made of red brick and have stone coping and banding. The piers support heavy iron carriage gates. There are two of them. Each is roughly six feet in width and eight feet in. On each side of the carriage gates are ornamental pedestrian gates that are roughly ten feet in height and three feet wide. The two outer gate piers are surmounted by friars' heads on the top that are roughly the same size as an actual human head. The two inner piers are surmounted by cast iron lamps. At the front of the pillars are engravings of "The Fall" and "Noah in the Ark." They were inspired by, and emulate those seen in Babylonian sculptures. Around the pillars are designs of the Heads of an **Angel**, a **Devil**, a **Sphinx, Dragons, a Flying Horse, Winged Serpents,** and other **Mythical Winged Beings.** There is also an engraving of a **Monster** with a woman's head and body and a bird's wings and claws. There are also engravings of reclining **Monks**, and all sorts of **bizarre faces**, some with their tongues sticking straight out. This is certainly an unusual way to design the entry gates to one's home.

The carriage gates open to allow three horse-drawn carriages to pass through, bringing with them members of your group who decided not to walk through the town as you had. Since they are arriving after you it makes you wonder just where they have been. Perhaps they made a detour to a local pub? Some people walk through the open gate, but you do not follow. Not yet. You have spent innumerable hours daydreaming about entering through these gates and seeing all the things that you have read and heard about. You have high expectations. This is not just another "walk in the park." This is an adventure. This is *your* adventure. Are you ready?

Wait. Don't rush forward just yet. Stay right where you are for another moment. Close your eyes. Take in a deep breath. Hold it for a moment. Now let it out slow. Open your eyes. The pedestrian gate is now wide open. You are about to cross the threshold. This is the moment you have been waiting for.

You are about to enter Friar Park.

Ye Lower Lodge

"Low but not Base"

You have just passed through one of the pedestrian gates that guards the grounds of Friar Park. Your feet are actually stepping upon the surface of the road that will bring you toward all the places you have thought about for so long. The first thing you see is an enchanting 1.5-story house on your left hand side. This new structure is referred to as the Lower Lodge. It was designed in a Flamboyant Gothic design style with red brick and stone-bands. The entire roof, with a plain ridge crest, is covered with rectangular clay tiles. The fiery red bricks and tiles, combined with the light stone bands, dressing, and gothic details stand in stark contrast to the green trees and blue sky behind it. This is actually the second version of this Lodge. Yes, there was another one here before this one. Because the owner was such a perfectionist who was not perfectly pleased with how it came out, he had it taken down and had this one - with a new design - put in its place. Does that seem a bit extreme to you? Perhaps it does, but it is standard practice of Frank Crisp who never hesitates building, and then taking down, or completely rebuilding any complete structure, portion of a structure, garden, man-made lake, or anything else he commissions, until it meets his lofty expectations.

    Directly in front of you is an octagonal-shaped room, with gothic-style, curvilinear-shaped, light stone mullions and transoms around double sets of tracery windows on each side of the exterior. Above the ground floor, on the corners, are eery and elongated gargoyles that spout out water from the above flat roof. Above that roof is a low, protective wall, along the edges of the balcony. Above that is a room, with the facade decorated in a red and white checkerboard pattern with brick and stone. Above that is a pyramidal, hexagonal-shaped roof divided by a whitestone frieze, with small windows that project vertically from a sloping roof. This

Built for Crisp's estate manager and head gardener.

portion of the roof is capped with a long, tall, iron finial that leans slightly to the side, giving the roof beneath it the appearance of a witch's hat. There is an ornate chimney stack with bands of bricks and white stone. The top is surrounded with mini carvings of faces of Friars and floral designs, along the top and the base. At the head of the stack is a decorative terracotta chimney pot. From this vantage point you see that the house is cross-gabled and there are at least six other ornate chimney stacks capped with terracotta pots toward the north and west sides of the house. Taking a few steps back, you can see that there is a gabled room on the far left with Tudor-style, exposed wood beams and stucco.

Take a few steps forward, you can take in a wide view of the east side of the Lower Lodge. Starting at the roof, there is a gabled dormer window that easily offers anyone upstairs a view of the front gate. Looking down, toward the bottom of the gable, you see that there is a room connecting to the octagonal-shaped structure. It has a flat roof with an ornate, low stone wall that matches the one that surrounds the balcony above the southeastern portion of the house. Now this is where things begin to get very unusual. There are intricate details carved into the facades of the lower lodge. Along the bottom of the windows is a band of light stone with LATIN sayings inscribed into it. The words are engraved on the design of a scroll, surrounded by decorative motifs. There is a puzzle to be solved here. Here is how to solve it. You need to start off on the lower word, and then read the upper word, and then read the lower word, and then read the upper word, and so on. But before you read the upper word, you are going to have to insert the word SUB – S-U-B - in order for this to make sense. What would you do that for? Simple! Because the Latin translation of the word SUB is the word UNDER.

Ye Lower Lodge

Translated to English, it translates as follows:

**"Oh crafty one, why do you cheat?
I discern that you will be suddenly destroyed,
for God raises up the lowly, but casts down those who deceive."**

Why on earth did Frank Crisp have that mysterious sentence inscribed into the wall? There may have been many reasons, but if you look at the shrubs around you, you can see that wire has been placed around them to keep visitors from cutting through in order to get to the front door. Perhaps that is Crisp's way of telling visitors like you to follow the gravel path to the front door, and not to cheat by cutting through the bushes.

Since you are now at the front door you may want to take a good look at it. To reach it you must walk up one stone step to a landing, and then turn right, and walk up two more steps, and then reach a landing to a porch within an entry way framed in gothic stone designs. On the corner post, overlooking the stairs, there is an engraving of a Friar that looks like a Fox. Above the porch, on the east side, is a Latin inscription that translates to:

"Humility without humiliation"

Walking further up the driveway, you see there is a room on the right hand side of the entry. In the center of it is a multi-pane traceried window beneath the same gable as the front door. Looking up along the top floor beneath the peak of the gable that has dark bargeboard with decorative details, there are two gothic-style windows framed in stone. Beneath them are six engraved designs under gothic arches. One of the engravings is that of a Friar known as the WINE FRIAR. He is depicted holding a cup and a tilted bottle of wine under the arched window to the left. Under the right side window, there is an engraving of a Friar holding a loaf of bread in his hand. He is known as the BREAD FRIAR. On each side of the engravings of Friars are decorative motifs. Under the Bread and Wine Friars is a Latin inscription of a biblical proverb that translates to:

"Come, eat of my bread and drink of the wine which I have mingled"

Frank Crisp wants visitors to be assured that it was WISDOM, and not physical refreshment, that the wealthy and wise King Solomon of Israel was referring to.

As you continue on, you pass the Lower Lodge, but before you do, you take a quick glimpse of the north side of it. There is a driveway here that

Above photo taken from within the grounds of Friar Park. The entry gates are on the far left, concealed behind the trees and shrubs.

is clearly for the private use of the resident of the Lower Lodge. The top floor has a charming little dormer window on the gabled room, with arched windows. There is an engraving of a Friar who is depicted as watching the Owner's Hearse passing and chuckling in the mood of the Latin inscription beneath it, which translates to:

"No footsteps backwards—for you"

That seems a bit morbid, but Frank Crisp clearly has an unusual sense of humor, and some have said, an eccentric personality. To your left is a dense, leafy wall of Golden Privet. It's bright golden foliage is thriving in this spot where it gets full sun. Along side of it are green-leaved plants which offer a pleasant contrast. In the Fall the foliage will take on a purple-red tone.

Ye Road to Ye Friar's Abode

You are standing upon the driveway that leads from the entry gates & the lower lodge to the mansion at Friar Park. You have travelled 500 feet up the paved way that is nearly wide enough for two horse-drawn carriages to pass one another. At this point the road veers left for another 500 feet until it veers right and heads straight north for nearly 400 feet until it reaches the front entry of the mansion.

But you are still quite a distance from approaching the house and that is perfectly fine because the story of this driveway is a lot more interesting than you may think. You see, in 1890 a very well-known book was written that discussed in great detail that this is more than just a road to travel upon by foot or hoof. It is indeed an approach route through an enclosed estate that is worthy of artistic treatment. Many English country homes have a straight drive with a stately avenue of trees toward an imposing structure. But here we have an undulating landscape so there are long, easy and graceful curves along artificial and natural slopes. New and tempting views are offered as the main drive rises gradually as it approaches its destination, while plantings of trees continue to shut off the view of the mansion itself until the driveway straightens up and offers the beautiful view ahead with no distractions of other buildings or pretty gardens.

Driveway was once compacted dirt, and then gravel, and was eventually paved.

Meet Mr. Knowles

By invitation, you have just passed through one of the pedestrian gates at the south entry to Friar Park. You are ascending the driveway. Whenever visitors pass the Lower Lodge they often wonder who enjoys the opportunity to live there. It certainly seems rather elaborate to simply offer shelter to whoever is guarding the gate. Obviously it is not the main house of the estate. It certainly was not built as a home for Frank Crisp's mother-in-law or any of his other relatives.

So, who is the fortunate lady or fellow who joyfully gets to call this storybok structure their home? Well, as a matter of fact, you can see him right now. He is standing along the left side of the driveway up ahead, smoking a pipe, and looking at you with a smile and offering a casual wave. He is being approached by a few visitors who have arrived before you. That is Mr. Philip Oswin Knowles. He seems to be a bit less than 6 feet tall. He is wearing black shoes, black pants, and a gray coat. He has a pasty white complexion, and has a walrus-type mustache with whiskers that are thick, and bushy, and droop over his mouth. Atop his head is a boater hat with a solid, ribbed, fabric ribbon around the crown. He works for Frank Crisp. He is in the position of being the property manager and the gardener who oversees Friar Park. Mr. Knowles is standing next to a table with a stack of crates.

As you approach you hear him tell some of the visitors that Friar Park's grounds and gardens are open to visitors one day – sometimes two days - each week, from the beginning of May until the end of September. This does not include special occasions such as this annual outing of the Horticultural Club. But no matter what, there is a charge to visitors of sixpence to access the property. But this money does not go to the wealthy owner of this fine estate. Oh, no! Not at all.

Above: What is the secret behind this optical illusion?

Mr. Crisp

Mr. Knowles

It is well-known, and appreciated, that half of all the proceeds are given to the Gardeners' Royal Benevolent Institution, and the other half to the Mayor of Henley for the assistance of the local charities. So everyone who visits is happy to pay the entry fee; knowing the money goes to good causes. Mr. Knowles is clearly a great source of wisdom. Who better than he to offer information on this strange new world than this man who is the mentor for the gardening staff? But more than just a source of knowledge he is also a valuable patron, who is in the possession of gifts and guides for those embarking on this adventure. In the crates beside him are special guides for visitors and colorful maps.

The pages of the visitors guides offer information that is needed to help understand this special world during your visit. The interior of the map includes a list of points of interest. Taking a quick glimpse at it, you understand why Friar Park has been described as having a "museum of gardens." Indeed it certainly does appear to be just that. After speaking with Mr. Knowles for while, he wishes you well upon your journey, and assures you that he will be wandering the grounds later and that he just might be around if and when he is needed.

Once you pass Mr. Knowles you come across another table. This one is beneath a wide tent and is covered with a patterned white cloth with frills

Meet Mr. Knowles

along its side. Atop it are pitchers and glasses of water, lemonade, and tea. Many people are gathered around it, some of whom are recuperating a bit from their journeys on their way in and out of the estate while exchanging gossip and sharing knowledge with new and existing friends. Here you will stop for a few moments and join the others, and refresh yourself before continuing on the mysterious road that awaits you ahead, within the grounds at Friar Park.

Don't Keep off the Grass

The driveway begins to climb in a northwest direction, overlooking lawns, trees and shrubs on both sides of you. On the lawn to your right is a sign that is surrounded by flowers. The sign is made of wood and is roughly three feet in width. On it are engraved words that say:

"DON'T KEEP OFF THE GRASS"

The sign was placed here by Frank Crisp who has quite a peculiar sense of humor. Legend has it that some visitors have been so confused by this sign that some actually stop in their tracks and go looking for the gardener in order to ask if the grass can, indeed, be walked upon. Or not.

Yes, it is okay for you to walk on the grass.

As the driveway turns you can stop and see the beautiful collection of Scarlet Oaks that seem to be at least 50 ft. tall. Their spreading canopy blocks sunlight and adds beauty to this landscape.

While looking up you see that large songbirds, squirrels, and white-tailed deer love to eat the acorns. These trees were likely brought over from the eastern United States.

You start walking again and you see that to your right there is a path that leads into an area that the vintage Friar Park map refers to as Ye Gloomie Glenne.

Travel notes:
This sign can be seen on the right side of the driveway, just past the Lower Lodge, as the road begins to turn left.

Ye Gloomie Glenne

You are walking along a narrow foot path, between tall trees. You are in Ye Gloomie Glenne. The path descends down on an ever deepening angle as the ground rises up around you. You are no longer even with the turf. You are entering a small, narrow, U-shaped gorge, with layers of fallen leaves upon the ground. This feels incredibly secluded as the steep walls of clinging soil become more sheer, and are now as high as your head. There are tall trees on either side of you, and the path is strewn with exposed tree roots. This certainly is rather dark, creepy, and gloomy. But there is a joy in being in this sort of environment. There is no one else around. Just the sounds of the birds on the branches, and the wind blowing through and around the trees and the occasional branch falling to the ground.

You look around at the exposed tree roots that are searching for every ounce of moisture they can absorb. Standing here in this solitude, this natural paradise, you can almost see the roots growing, though you know that would be barely perceivable. Yet, here you are, and you can hear your own breathing, you can feel every inch of your skin, you can feel every drop of sunlight that struggles to break through the canopy above to reach the forest floor where you are, and you feel at home. A sense of calmness consumes you. There is no place to rush to. There are no calls to make. There is no one to see today. This is your time. These are your moments. They belong to you, and no one can take them away.

So you stand here, and you look around, and you are surrounded by trees., and there are walls of green leaves around you. This is the first gift Friar Park has given to you.

At this point, there is no way of knowing what else awaits you within Friar Park. There is no way of knowing what awaits you in an hour, in the afternoon, this evening, tomorrow, or anytime in the future. As far you are concerned, being where you are, right now, surrounded by trees - none of it matters.

So clear your mind because in this area of Friar Park ... time stands still, and so do you. So just stand still. And stay here as long as you like. You are safe. The trees are protecting you.

Travel Notes:
Because the path descends down, be careful following it after a heavy rain, or as the snow is melting, because the soil can be very damp and soggy.

Ye Small Birdies Paradise

As you exit you look up and see an assortment of trees, with leaves that have vibrant colors radiating in the bright sunlight. This area is known as Ye Small Birdies Paradise. Looking up, you can see and hear a wide variety of birds. Over the course of time the following birds could be seen in, around, and above Friar Park:

Blackbirds, Blackcap, Bullfinch, Buzzard, Carrion Crow, Chaffinch, Collard Dove, Cuckoo, Dunnock, Fieldfare, Garden Warbler, Goldcrest, Goldfinch, Great Spotted Woodpecker, Green Woodpecker, Greenfinch, House Martin, House Sparrow, Jackdaw, Jay, Magpie, Meadow Pipit, Merlin, Mistle Thrush, Nuthatch, Pheasant, Pied Wagail, Red Kites, Red-legged Partridge, Redwing, Ring-Necked Parakeet, Robin, Siskin, Skylark, Song Thrush, Sparrowhawk, Starling, Stock Dove, Swallow, Swift, Tawny Owl, Tree Sparrow, Willow Warbler, Wood Pigeons, Wren, and Yellow Hammer.

Travel notes:
Remember to walk slowly while listening to the spectacular sounds of the singing birds. Perhaps sit down and lean against a tree, close your eyes, and cast your mind back into a more leisurely time. There is so much to learn from quiet moments you can spend alone, with chirping birds and falling leaves.

Ye Alpine Meadow

There is a wide blue sky above you and you come upon a wide open field to your right that is planted with flowers. This area is known as Ye Alpine Meadow. Before Frank Crisp purchased this property the area in front of you was not a valley at all, with banks on either side, and undulations of the ground.

The old conditions, Frank Crisp had said, was entirely obliterated. In fact there was once a belt of trees in the foreground that shut out views of the distance. So the trees were removed. But even then the surface was uninteresting. So the grounds were scooped out and shaped and converted into a valley to show the scenery to the best advantage. This is "landscape gardening" as it was originally understood, and implemented by such gifted landscape architects as the great Lancelot Brown, also known as Capability Brown, in England, in the mid-late 1700s. A flower-rich bed has been planted within this man-made meadow, which creates a natural environment in order for them to flourish. Among the plants spreading in the area are: Cuckoo Flowers with four pink petals, Ragged Robins, with its pink flowers that have tasty nectar that butterflies and long-tongued bees like to feed on. Marsh Marigolds, with brightly colored yolk-yellow flowers that produce both nectar and copious amounts of pollen which attract many insect visitors. Over there are tall specimens of dark pink Southern Marsh Orchids. The meadow is also bursting with Drooping Bluebells, with recurved petals. There is also a harvest of flowering Yellow Rattle. The bumblebees are having a grand ol' time visiting the Red and White Clovers. Over there are Cornflowers with grey-green branched stems. They seem to be at least two-feet tall. The flower heads are an intense blue color. That annual plant will flower all summer-long. No wide field is complete without some Poppies. There are an assortment of colors here and they are in full bloom! There are even some deep pink Corn Cockles. Toward the far end are 3 ft. tall Oxeye Daisies. The leaves are dark green with small flower heads, consisting of white ray florets that surround a yellow disc. Black Medick, with three leaflets and a small, yellow flower, grouped in bunches. There are also some ivy-leaved Toadflax growing on rocks. In the foreground are yellow-flower Oxford Ragwort. Sprawling stems of Scarlet Pimpernel flowers are toward the back, with their bright green, soft leaves, and colorful symmetrical flowers. The area is further enlivened by deep pink Spotted Orchids. There are also beautiful clumps of Butterfly Weed with electric orange flowers that attract butterflies. Look! There are even some Hummingbirds enjoying the sweet nectar.

As you walk further you see a solitary tree that is surrounded by a trunk-hugging, roundabout bench. But it is too early in your journey to take a break yet so you keep on strolling upon a path within Friar Park.

Travel notes: The flowers are for viewing and not for the taking, so leave them be, to grow in the sunlight to their full potential. If anything, you may reach out your hand and softly touch their soft petals. Take in some deep breaths and enjoy the open space around you.

Ye Stone of Precation

On the right side of the driveway, about 500 ft from the entry gates, is a large stone with the following inscription carved into it:

"Be kindly wanderer through this garden's ways.
Nor let thine indignation prompt thy hand
To cast revengeful stones, because perchance
An imperfection thou hast found.
Some flower Laid low or wan;
some tree bearing no fruit;
Some scene o'er wrought;
some theme thy whim abhors;
Some strange defect thy skill would ne'er let be.
The gardener toiled to make his garden fair.
Most for thy pleasure."

Frank Crisp "liberated" those lines from the dedication page of a book entitled, The Mystic Rose from the Garden of the King, written by Fairfax L. Cartwright, Sr., and published in 1898.

Basically, Crisp meant to convey that if you see some parts of the garden that are not perfect, just let it go, and enjoy it for what it is.

Ye Waye Throughe Ye Woode

Standing upon the driveway that the map refers to as **Ye high waye to ye Friar's abode**, you see **Ye stone of precation** to your right, alongside a northward path named **Ye path of ye South poole**. Turning to your left, you walk southward upon the grass with a series of tall evergreen trees to your left, until you come upon a path known as **Ye waye through ye woode**. It is indeed a miniature woodland walk. You take your time as you enjoy hearing the muffled sounds of your shoes walking upon the compacted earth and gravel path that meanders a bit north, and then east, and then south, with tall evergreen trees on either side of you, as you follow it south until it curves back up, in a northerly direction, and then you come across the series of coniferous trees that have blue-green colored needles to your left. They have scaly grey bark on their trunks with brownish-yellow branches. Gosh, they are tall! They seem to be nearly 50 ft. high with densely growing horizontal branches. You follow the path southward until you come across more well-trimmed grass where the path ends. All together the path was about 225 ft. in length. Looking to your left you see more of the ornamental trees with the blue-green colored needles as you walk toward the driveway, just west of where the path splits and leads to **Ye Gloomie Glenne**. But since you've already been there, you start walking northwest once again, as you continue your grand tour of Friar Park.

Ye Place for Ye Calme Reflexion

You are seated upon the cool, thin grass just off the driveway, to the west of **Ye pathe of ye Southe poole** and **Ye stone of precation**. Directly in front of you is **Ye Southe poole**. The area where you are seated is known as **Ye place for ye calme reflexion**.

Looking along the edges of the lake you see an assortment of Primula plants with clusters of flowers on the spherical centers of their stout stems. Some of the flowers are **purple**, while others are **yellow**, and some are **rose**-colored, and other are in shades of **pink**, and there are even some flowers that are in shades of **blue**, and in the distance you see some that are **white** and shades of **scarlet** and **cream**.

Along the paths and to the north and east are numerous trees, many of which were here for many years, and many have been newly planted, including Blue Colorado Spruce.

From here you watch a family of mallard ducks leisurely waddle upon the surface of the sparkling water, near a couple of dabbling mute swans with pure white plumage, and you observe a Red Squirrel rushing up a tree trunk to the safety of a branch with a little delicacy in its mouth, and you lean back and feel the warm sun rays land upon your face as your head sinks back into the cool blades of grass as you drift away into your dreams as a warm wind blows above and around you.

Glancing up you see a tall Field Maple with a large, dense, round-shaped crown that is filled with birds. It has olive-colored leaves, svelte light-brown twigs and deeply-furrowed dark brown bark. Its flowers are small, yellow-green, cup-shaped and are

hanging in clusters of one to two dozen.
There are other trees with ball-shaped flowers and bristly fruits. Many of the trees have evergreen needles and leaves. Growing along the waterside is a broad-leafed Crack Willow. You watch and listen as one of its branches snaps and falls to the ground. A bit further away is a majestic English Elm with a fan-shaped crown. The leaves are dark green and the bark is light grey brown, rough and fissured. It has leaves that are round to oval, and toothed with a rough, hairy surface. The flowers are dark pink to red and are hanging in tassels. Over there you can see a European Holly with smooth branchlets, glossy, dark-emerald leaves and bright-red berries. Legend has it that Holly trees can be used as a charm against witches and goblins, which must please the Gnomes at Friar Park quite a bit! In fact, perhaps they are the ones who planted it. One never knows in a place such as this, where anything and everything is possible and magical.

Ye Water Lilies

As you continue walking forward along the driveway, you see the southern portion of the lake on your right hand side. As you approach you see a small, calm inlet in full-sun where colorful and vibrant water lilies happily float upon, and spread across, the warm water's surface.

Such lush foliage! Some of the leaves are soft while others are jagged, but all are round, with a radial notch. The assortment of colors of the elegant flowers are like a showy display of jewels reflecting off of the surface of the pond. **Yellow! Pink! Red! White! Purple! Blue! Orange!**

Such a variety of shapes, too! There are some that are star-shaped and cup-shaped, while others are pointed, and some are even fluffy. Each waxy cuticle allows rain water to quickly roll off the surface so that the leaves do not sink.

The designers of this lake created this small body of water where much of the plants are submerged and are rooted in the mud at the bottom. In addition to their beauty, their shapes and shade give shelter to small fish in the pond, as well as for frogs. In fact, there are a few hopping along right now! Their flowers also provide early nectar for insects.

Friar Park is filled with many spectacular sights, but every area offers opportunities for calm, and reflection, and beauty, including this little pond filled with water lilies. So stay where you are for as many moments as you like, and take in a deep breath, and enjoy the fantastic fragrance of the fabulous flowers.

Ye Shamrock Garden & Tea House

You are walking up the driveway at Friar Park. On your right is a stone path that, according to the map, leads to **Ye Sham-Rock Garden**. What shall you do at this point? Walk forward or turn right? It's not too difficult of a decision, is it? So you walk off the driveway, and on to the grass, and then on to a series of stepping stones. You slowly follow them around to the north end of this garden, to the left of the pool filled with Water Lilies.

Keeping your eyes to your left, and not toward the body of water to your right or in front of you, you see a **Japanese Tea House** on a cliff opposite a ravine and a bridge. There is also a narrow brook and a series of waterfalls that are clearly of artificial construction, but they look very realistic, indeed!

At the north end of the steps there is a Torii, which, as you know, is a traditional Japanese gate most commonly found at the entrance of, or within, a Shinto shrine, where it symbolically marks the transition from the profane to the sacred. So, why is this called a **Sham-Rock** garden? That seems like an unusual name considering the Japanese theme? Perhaps the word Sham-Rock is actually a compound word that was designed to confuse people. The definition of "Sham"

is a thing that is not what it is purported to be. Rather than being a garden filled with three-leaf clovers, or having any sort of Irish theme, it seems that instead it is a garden filled with rocks that were man-made of crushed bricks and cement; thereby making them "sham" rocks. Either way it sure is quite lovely.

Glancing around, you see a wooden bench that overlooks the water, and you stop and sit for a moment and watch as an assortment of 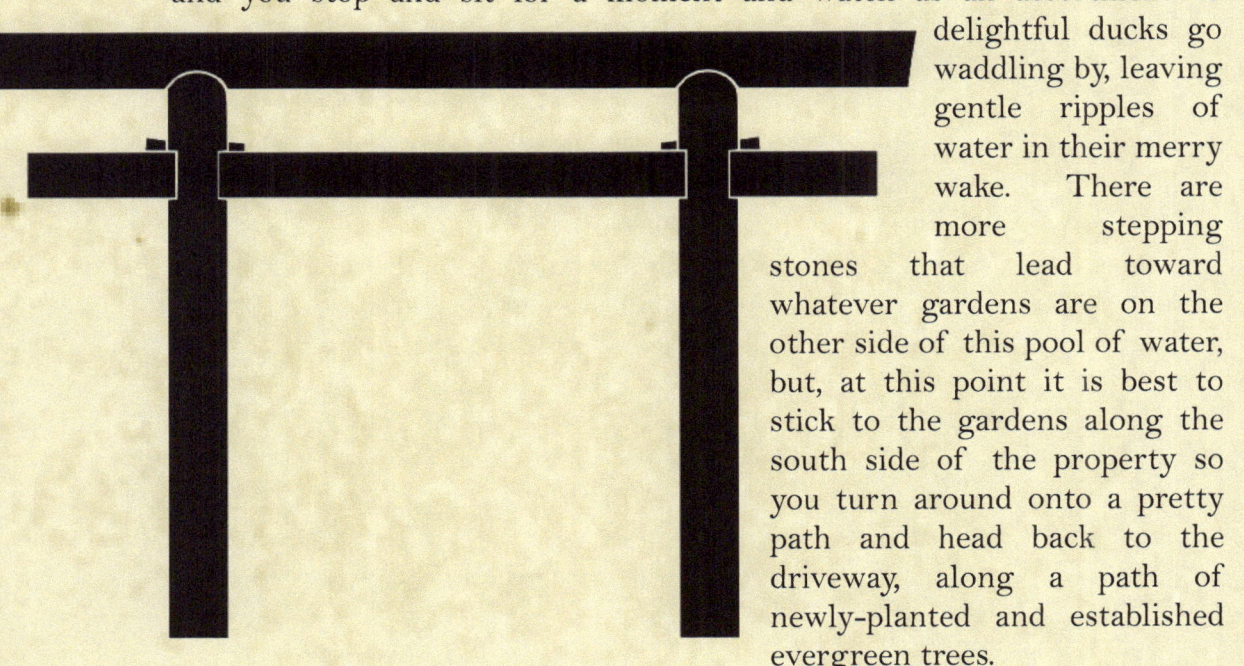 delightful ducks go waddling by, leaving gentle ripples of water in their merry wake. There are more stepping stones that lead toward whatever gardens are on the other side of this pool of water, but, at this point it is best to stick to the gardens along the south side of the property so you turn around onto a pretty path and head back to the driveway, along a path of newly-planted and established evergreen trees.

Ye Middle Lodge

"In ye middle ye will go safest"

You are walking westward on the driveway, within the grounds of Friar Park, until you come across a bit of an intersection. You have three choices at this point. 1) You can continue forward on the driveway, or 2) you can turn right, on a footpath that leads to a large bed of blooming flowers, or 3) you can turn left.

Being that you are still so close to the southern perimeter of the property it does not seem that there would be much reason to turn left, until you see along a short spur path, roughly 60 feet away, a charming 1.5 story structure that looks strikingly similar to the Lower Lodge. Looking at the map, you see that this structure is referred to as **Ye Middle Lodge**.

You turn left onto a gravel path and begin to approach it. You then come across another path that leads to your left. It is **Ye Longe Walke of Coole and Shade** that leads back to where you started. You do not want to do that, so you keep walking forward - and there it is! The Middle Lodge. It has been built of red bricks with stone dressings with cross gables covered with a clay tile roof in the familiar flamboyant gothic style. For the benefit of privacy there are some mature trees on your right concealing the back of the house, and there are trees on the other side of the path to your left.

Before looking at the house you check out the flower beds that, according to the Visitors' Guide, were arranged based upon an illustration Frank Crisp saw in a book that was published in the year 1614. The gravel pathway is made of crushed quarry tile and is lined with horizontal bricks on both sides. It leads straight ahead to a pedestrian gate that leads to the

street and to the front door. Clearly this is a guest house. It is a magnificent one! To your right is a small lawn of grass, and gardens, and some box hedges. The first part of the house you come across is a square-shaped, triple aspect room with north, south, and west facing views. Each side has arch-shaped casement windows with transoms above, all within elaborate, light stone moldings. Above is a flat roof with a low, protective, and decorative light stone wall along the edge of the perimeter. Clearly this is a balcony that can be accessed from the top floor. Standing at the part of the path where you can approach the door you are able to get a full view of the entire east facade. There is a water fountain surrounded by a circle of flowers on the lawn on the left side of the path. In the center is a round headed arch entry with multiple stone moldings that leads to an inner hall with a door with multi-pane leaded glass in the center. There is a doorbell attached to the brick wall on the right between two stone bands. On the left side is a stone buttress that is as tall as the top of the doorway. Above the entry is a frieze with an engraving that was inspired by French daredevil acrobat Charles Blondin (who had died in 1897). He had gained fame as the first person to walk across Niagara Falls on a tightrope. so the engraving is referred to as a **"Blondin" Friar"**. It is that of a Friar walking on tight rope. Beneath it is a latin inscription that translates to:

"In the middle you will go most safely"

or

"The Middle Course"

Ye Middle Lodge

Clearly this is in reference to the fact that this is the **Middle Lodge**. Some of Frank Crisp's puzzles are easier to decipher than others. The entry to the lodge has been incorporated into the base of a tower that has a red and white checkerboard pattern toward the top with one (1) deep-set miniature, stone, arch-shaped window on each side. Above that are clay tiles on a shallow, inclining roof, and then the dark wood frames of an open-air porch with two rectangular windows on each side, allowing all encompassing views of every side of the Lodge. Above that is a pyramidal-shaped roof covered in red clay tiles. It is then capped at the top with a tall copper finial.

To the left of the entry is an elaborate, east-facing square bay with three multi-paned tracery windows and transoms with stone mullions, and a stone hood moulding at the top. Above is dark bargeboard beneath a gabled and polychromatic-tiled roof with alternating rectangular and fish-tail shingles. Best of all, there is a terra-cotta, gothic-themed dragon finial clinging to a segmental, cross-ridge tile at the peak of the gable's end, looking directly down upon you from high above. Judging from here it seems to be perhaps 10 inches wide and 19 inches in length and about 12 inches high with a wing span of perhaps 12.5 inches. Most of the east facade is red brick, laid up in common bond with just a few bands of light stone beneath the gable. As mentioned previously there is a path leading to an iron gate that heads out to Gravel Hill. The gate is supported by stone banded piers. On each side is an iron wall with intricate iron cresting atop a low wall with brick and stone banded piers.

As of today the low wall consists of dark bricks laid up, 4 or 5 high, in common bond and a band of white stone, and then a wall of red bricks, laid up 5 high, in common bond with stone coping atop, and an ornate security fence. From Gravel Hill you can view the south side of the Middle Lodge. It is here where you can see that this section is cross gabled with a pair of red brick and light stone banded chimneys, topped with terra-cotta pots. On the southeast corner is a stone buttress that leads up to a stone pinnacle. Starting from the top you get a good view of the triple, high-arch crest tiles along the ridge of the gables with the dragon gargoyle on the right side. In the center is a high peaked cross-gable. The gables are covered with alternating, polychromatic rectangular and fishtail slate shingles. Beneath the steeply pitched peak is a dark bargeboard and ornamental milled panels with decorative details that are fastened to the projecting gable. Beneath that are four decorative medallions, and beneath that are four casement windows with decorative glass surrounded by fish-tale slate shingles. From here you get a great view of the decorative chimney stacks with their fantastic brickwork. The flue is encased with a terra-cotta pot topped with a terracotta Chimney cowl. The room beneath the gable juts out above the ground floor and is secured by red brackets.

To the left is a cast iron gutter and down pipe. In the center are three gothic, arched-shaped, leaded glass windows with transoms above, all within stone moldings. To the right, on the ground floor, is a frieze with decorative motifs. Beneath that are two elaborately carved arched window casements with a rose design on the top of the leaded glass panes.

Let's walk west, along the path to view the west side of the house. From here you see that there are two asymmetrical gables capped with bun and peg finials. On the peak of the northeast side of the back gable is an elegant swan neck ridge finial. There are two casement windows with leaded lights under the right side gable, closest to the road. There is a brick-walled courtyard in the back with walls that are 10-12 ft high.

Now that you have seen most of the Middle Lodge you can turn back around and walk back to the driveway before you veered off in this direction. As you walk back it is interesting to know that over the course of time the Middle Lodge was mainly used as a guest cottage. Following the death of Mr. Crisp, this cottage was rented to someone not in the household. When George Harrison purchased Friar Park, he and his wife Pattie Boyd stayed at the Middle Lodge while the house itself was renovated.

Once George Harrison installed his recording studio, some of the musicians who recorded there, would stay at the Middle Lodge.

Ye Longe Walke of Coole & Shade

To the south of the Middle Lodge is a long, arrow path with a thick carpet of leaf litter, just over 700 feet in length, called **Ye Longe Walke of Coole and Shade**. To the right, blocking the sites and sounds of people and horses and carriages along Gravel Hill, are rows of evergreen trees. To your left is a wide open view of the driveway and lake to the north. In fact, it is here where you come across a wooden bench where the map says, **Here maye ye rest awhile.**

Among the trees, within the dense canopy, ablaze in the autumn air, are mature European Beech - each with their own many-branched dome - that are nearly 100 feet tall. Small, roughly triangular, and edible Beechnuts are found in

small burs beneath and around your feet.

There are also Scots Pine, with long, bare and straight trunks topped with masses of foliage. You approach one and look at the thick, scaly dark grey-brown bark on the lower trunk. Looking up you see thin, flaky and warm-orange bark on the upper trunk and branches. The bark will continue to fissure as these trees age for hundreds of years. Looking down you see pale brown cones on the ground.

Here also can be found the tallest broad-leaved tree in Britain. The Common Linden with dark green, heart-shaped leaves with drawn-out pointed tips which are a favorite of sap-sucking insects. Other insects are feasting on the nectar and pollen. It's sweetly scented, yellowish-white flowers are attracting bunches of buzzing honey bees.

Of course there are also some English Oak trees that seem to be about 50 feet high with wide trunks, rugged, crooked branches and their wide, expansive crowns.

Look up and see shiny brown, one-inch long acorns attached to long stalks next to leaves that are blue-green above and lighter beneath, and have ear-like lobes at the base.

A little bit south of this point are the tall evergreen trees that conceal **Ye Waye Through ye Woode.**

Continuing eastward the path leads through rows of trees on either side, creating a shady canopy as you follow it all the way to the left side of the Lower Lodge near the entry gates.

Where ye Echo Lays

You are now back on the driveway. You turn left and the road begins to ascend. After a few moments the driveway begins to veer right, heading north, and a cool mist begins to descend down in every direction. Strangely enough the air suddenly feels chilled. The heavy pale-white fog seems to have wrapped itself around you. Looking in every direction it seems as if a cloud has fallen to the ground and you are in the middle of it. Looking down, you can barely see your feet. Looking up, you can barely see your hands outstretched in front of you. Your visibility has decreased substantially. This is quite a mystery. Just remain calm and don't walk too quickly in any direction. After all, you do not want to accidentally walk off the driveway and into a tree branch, or trunk, or tumble down a ravine.
Stay still and gather your thoughts. Now just take just a few careful steps forward. As you do you feel cool moisture upon your face. Now the thick fog seems to be thinning. Looking up you see patches of the blue sky, and then the burning bright golden hue of the sun. Looking back in the direction you were facing you see the faint view of something in a red color tone in the distance. It is beginning to take shape. The fog is dissipating. Yes! There it is! At the end of this broad driveway, about 100 feet in front of you, is the fantastical facade of Friar Park's magnificent mansion. You are not dreaming. You are really here - at the mansion! This is going to be great. There is so much to see here at Friar Park.

Ye Friar's Abode

You are standing in front of the magnificent mansion. Wow. It is like something out of a fantasy story. Where and how does one begin describing what is before you? Stand still. Don't move. Just close your eyes and take in a deep breath and let it out slowly. You can feel yourself sinking a little bit down into the gravel. It's like you are shifting into another dimension where fairies and dragons and mysterious and magical things are everywhere. You have heard so many stories about this startling structure. Where do the myths begin and where do the legends end? You have heard that around the interior and exterior of the house are carvings in the shapes of monks – usually in a mocking fashion. Some are short fat monks with long habits, and others are tall skinny monks with short habits. Could that really be true? Why on earth would such carvings even exist? It's a mystery! But now you are truly here. And this is your chance to determine what *is* real, what is *not* real, and what is *un*real.

Taking in a grand overview, this is an incredibly large house. The entire facade is roughly 130 ft. across. It is built of red-brick with horizontal stone bands, dressings, and trimming in a flamboyant gothic style. The roof has multiple, asymmetrical cross-gables, and steeply pitched towers and turrets with pyramidal shaped roofs. All are covered in rectangular red tiles. There are numerous sets of very tall and thin chimney stacks, designed in ornate, symmetrical patterns, with bands of colored cut bricks and light stone, and capped with terracotta pots and cowls.

In the background is a hexagonal tower with a pyramidal roof above an open-air porch that seems to be a bell tower, or a watch tower, above red brick. In the very forefront is a high gable with a rose designed window frame in white stone. What stands out the most about the south side facade are

gothic-style, tracery windows, with elaborately carved, geometrically shaped stone moldings. In addition to allowing a great deal of light to enter the mansion, the numerous windows help break up the vast walls of red brick and light stone of the fantastic facade.

You are standing directly in front of the entry. Before you get to that, look toward the far left side of the south facade and work your way in. At the far end are two-story and three-story sections with additional chimney stacks towering over the roofs. Toward the center is a wide space projecting outward from the main walls of the building and forming a rounded bay in the room on the other side. The bay is roughly 20 ft. in width. Each of the three angles on both stories have three-light, gothic windows which means they have nine windows per floor. There is a stone balcony at the top that is accessed by large multi-paned glass doors within another bay window. Behind that is a red brick gable with a rounded peak.

The windows on the ground floor, and the two above it, have curvilinear tracery windows with stone mullions and transoms. To the right of that is a flat wall, roughly 15 ft. in width, with a tall, round-headed gothic-style tracery window that looks like something out of a cathedral, that allows light to enter into the staircase within. To the right, just to the left of the entry, are more gothic-style tracery windows along the 2nd floor. Along the ground floor is a room that extends out further than than the rest of the facade. It is roughly 20 ft. in width. It has a flat roof with a parapet along top with some battlements that add an ingenious look to this portion of the facade that has multiple stone arched windows that allow light to enter the toilets and the coat room on the other side. Beneath them, along the foundation, are small windows that allow light to enter the cellar.

Entry to ye Friar's Abode

The entry to the house begins with a double Tudor-shaped entry of stone below an elaborately carved balcony. At the sides and top of the stone entry are six reptilian gargoyles that look down upon all those who enter.

The width of the entryway, including the supporting columns, seems to be about 10 feet in width. But the double doors to actually enter the house itself are about 10 feet further in. Outside the main entrance is a carving of a friar holding a battered frying pan. The caption is:

"Two Holy Friars"

On the west side of the porch are carved sculptures that depicts a Friar and Satan. The Friar is only holding a book because the Devil took the bell and candle away from him. On the floor of the entry porch is a Latin inscription that translates as follows:

**"Tell not all you know.
He who tells all that he knows
often tells more than he knows."**

On the doorstep is the Chinese proverb:

"Every man should sweep the snow from his own door
and not worry about his neighbor's."

The Chronogram above Friar Park's main entry reveals the year 1895 as the date the house was first occupied and translates to:

"Welcome, friends,
As many as wish to enter;
Come in peace,
Eat, drink,
Live merrily,
In peace depart."

On each side of the front entry columns are carvings of frogs. On one side is a frog who has dropped into a vat of milk and who paddled away until it turned into butter and then the frog was able to escape. On the other side of this carving is a frog who was not that optimistic, and who did not even try, so you know what happened to him, right? He drowned. As you walk in further you can see the elaborately carved, double wooden doors within the Outer Hall. Carved in the panels of the doors are the heads of two nuns framed within two large bells. Above the door is a Latin inscription which has two meanings, depending upon the position of the comma. They translate as either:

"O door be open, be shut to no honest man."

Or

"O door be open to none, be shut to the honest man."

There are stone benches on either side of the entrance portico. The front face of each is a prison grill with the carved face of a friar behind it. On the floor are two scrapers. Each one is decorated with Friars holding whips. They have been placed here so that visitors can wipe the bottom of their shoes on the brushes. Now, look to your left and you will see the electric doorbell that is in the shape of a Friar's Head. To activate the bell one needs to pull the Friar's tongue which is made of a piece of bright green malachite. Now that you are at the front doors you would probably love to open them up and walk inside the house, wouldn' you? Be patient. We will get to that on another tour. So for now, just turn around and leave the Outer Hall so you can walk you over to the east side of the magnificent mansion at Friar Park.

East of ye Friar's Abode

You are standing in the broad driveway along the south side of the house. As you turn right and begin walking east you pass an ornamental stone BENCH on your right side. This is referred to as the SOUTH SEAT. On the opposite site is a Latin inscription that translates to:

"If you sit in your own seat who shall turn you out of it?"

Look around and you will notice that the house sits upon the highest point of land on the property, atop a plateau. It offers a grand view of the pleasure ground that descends down a slope. You are also able to take in a wide and unobstructed view above the tree tops of the east side of Henley toward and beyond the River Thames. You are standing on a gravel path that is roughly 10 ft. to 12 ft. in width and runs for roughly 150 ft. across the facade of the house. To your left, the grassy lawn extends out roughly 12 ft. from the house. To your right is another grassy area that extends out roughly 12 ft. until it reaches a low stone wall. On the other side of the stone wall is a descending slope that is roughly 15 ft. in width. From where you are standing, on your right, there is a semi-circle stone staircase that descends down in a slight curvature, 30 feet in length, to the **Terrace Garden**. Now walk straight up the path. Look closely and you will see that, like the south side, the east side of the House is made up of red bricks and light stone and includes carvings with mottoes, puzzles and inscriptions. Many of the puzzles or designs have double meanings. From here you see that the House is three stories high beneath the attic covered with rectangular red roof tiles. As you walk past the first set of windows on the ground floor you can see that the lower panes are clear and open out to this terrace while the transoms above are multi-paned stained glass. On the other

East of ye Friar's Abode

side is the Dining Room. Look up, toward the higher floors. You can see a stone sculpture of a monstrous-looking Friar that is depicted devouring two boys, while overhead is a Friar blessing what is going on down below.

Continue walking north and the second set of windows on your left are for the **Library Room**. This is a bay window that extends up to the second floor with an elaborately carved stone balcony. These also have tall, glass windows with stained glass transoms above and detailed designs carved in stone. Between the two bay windows are a set of stone pillars. They are embellished with decorative carvings and friezes leading all the way up to a Tudor arch on the third floor with elaborate stone carvings. There are no glass windows within the frames, because on the other side is a porch. There are carvings of monk faces on the top of each column. Above the ground floor windows you see sculptures of coins that represent the Empress Crispina, the wife of the brutal Emperor Commodus, and Crispus, the son of Constantine.

Continue walking north and the third set of windows on your left are for the **Library**'s adjoining **Study**. Keep walking until you reach the furthest part of the east side of the house. The sets of windows to your left are to the **Drawing Rooms**. Over the window of the Drawing Rooms are heads representing the Four Ages of Friar-hood – the boy, the youth, the middle-aged, and the old. Further along are engravings of two monkeys. One monkey is plainly visible. The other is left to be discovered by the observer. Then there is an oriel window at the very end. On the buttress is a design showing some cubes. If you count them over carefully, you will find only six, but, if you know how to solve the puzzle it can soon be proven to you that there are seven in all. The base of each cube is so drawn that the whole makes a complete optical illusion. On the same corner near these cubes are two segments of a circle, so placed that one appears much longer than the other. Yet, if you test them by measure, you will find that they are of the same length. And there are many other puzzles and optical illusions to look at, but you really must be moving on. There is so much more to see!

Now that you have reached the northernmost side of the east facade, close to another wide stone bench, turn right and walk away from the house a bit to take in a grand view of the entire east side. It seems to be roughly 135 feet in width. There are two bay windows on the ground floor. There are bay windows above them. There are six smallish dormer windows in the attic. There are also what appear to be two stone dormers above the windows, but they are actually doors that lead out to the stone balconies above the bay windows. There are three sets of red and yellow banded chimneys rising high above the attic. On the northern section the east side is only two stories high with a flat roof with a stone railing, that surrounds a large tiled porch.

But what stands out the most is the 80-foot high, square-shaped tower that rises to a pyramidal roof. It climbs up four stories from the ground, plus there is

76

an attic above, with narrow windows within the pyramidal shape that is capped with a copper finial. There is a round corner turret with a pyramidal roof on the left side and an octagonal corner turret with indentations reminiscent of battlements on the right side. It also has tall, narrow, stained glass windows with pointed arches at top called Lancets. In the center of it is a large pole with a weather-vane atop. Between them are three windows surrounded by stone. From this angle, you can see a flag on a pole waving high above the house.

Just like the south side of this facade where you began there is also a wide stone bench on this end of the path. On the back of it is a representation of a cowl, followed by Latin words that translate to:

"The cowl does not make the monk."

As you likely know, this is an age-old proverb. A cowl is a long cloak with a hood that covers the head of the wearer. The proverb means that the wearing of such a garment does not turn a man into a monk; he just may be a 'a wolf in sheep's clothing'. In other words, "The superficial trappings of something are unrelated to its true essence." On the seat itself is a Spanish proverb, that translates to:

"Give me where I may sit; I will make where I may lie down."

The meaning being that if you should kindly offer something to someone, he or she will ask for more from you the next time. The English equivalent being, "Give him an inch, and he will take a mile."

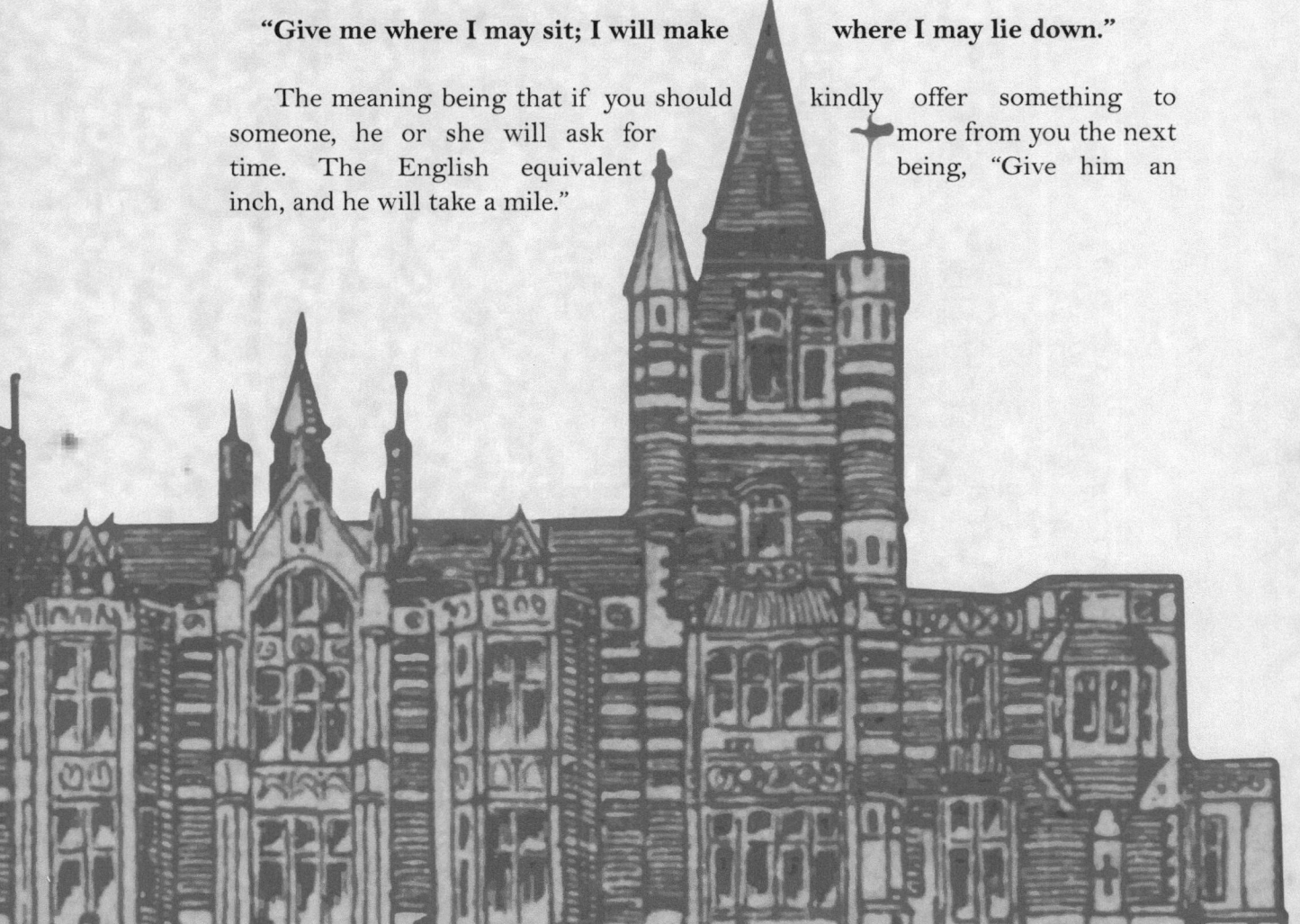

Ye Terrace Garden & Ye Fountain of Perpetual Mirth

You are standing at the northernmost end of the gravel path that runs along the east side of the House. There is a strong breeze coming in from the east that nearly blows you back a bit. You can smell the sweet perfume of flowers swirling around you. The sky is bright blue and birds are swooping down, circling, gliding, flapping, rising above, and flying in every direction. To your left is a stone staircase that leads down to the Terrace Garden below. You follow the steps down to the bottom.

The path you are now on, like the others in this area, are of finely-crushed pieces of brick, and the borders are of whole red bricks. The paths are roughy 7.5 ft wide. To your right is the grassy slope below the stone wall. To your left is an "Open Knot" Garden with formal beds mostly in a scroll form. The outer beds are roughly 12 ft. wide by 40 ft. long. They are planted with dwarf shrubs. The inner area is planted with violas in the winter and bedding-out plants in the summer. This type of garden is also referred to as a **Dutch Garden**," with the reason being that, according to most agreed-upon definitions:

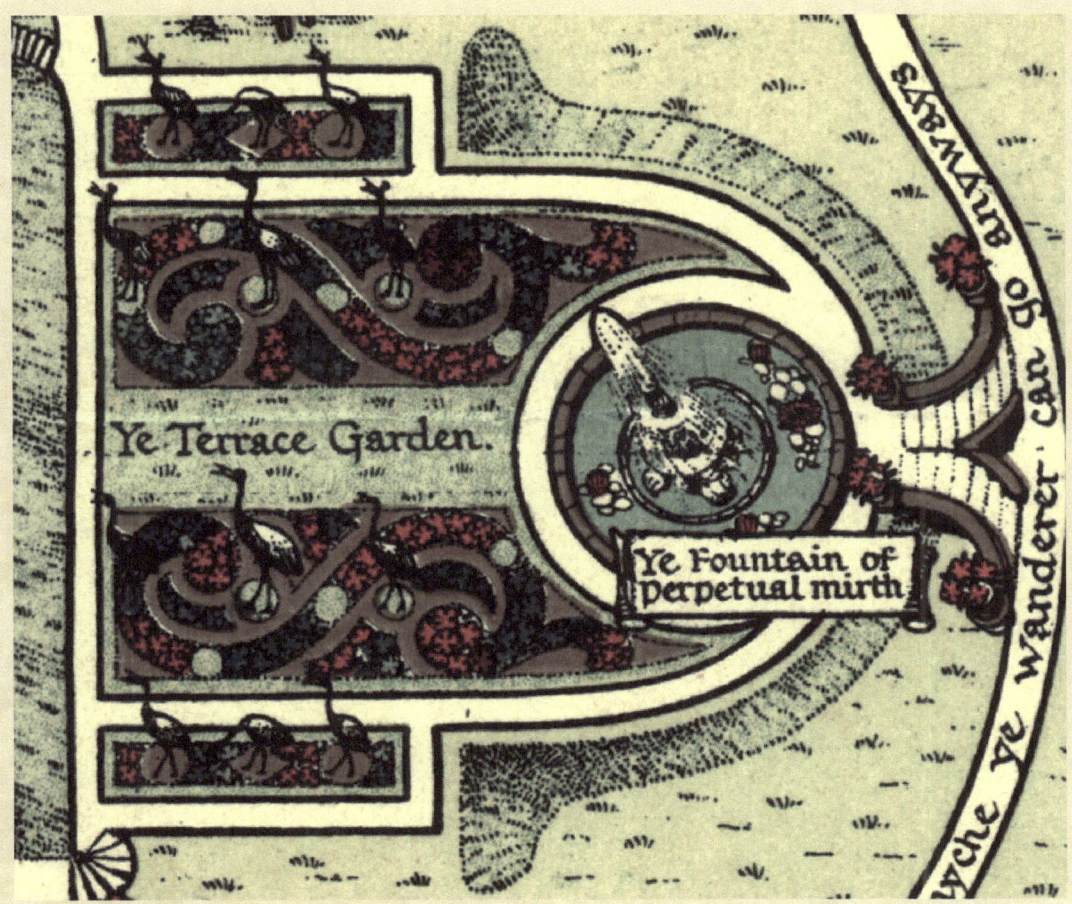

Dutch gardens are enclosed within hedges and the space within is laid out in a highly cultivated and geometrical, often symmetrical, fashion, shaped by dense plantings of highly colored flowers, and edged with box or other dense and clipped shrubs. They also sometimes include areas with fountains.

    All together this Terrace Garden is roughly 114 ft. in width by 93 ft. in length, extending out to the edge of the furthest path on the east side. Around the Terrace Garden are stone vases that are embellished with Friars' masks. They are filled with red, yellow and white flowering plants. You walk past the outer bed and then a path, and then you walk along the west side of a bed filled with scrolling hedges that is roughly 24 ft. in width. You then reach a wide and open grassy path down the center of the Terrace Garden. It is roughly 15 ft. wide and leads directly to a round stone fountain on the far side of the garden. The entire length from this spot to the fountain is roughly 47 ft. In the center is a stone urn filled with stunning red roses.

    You now approach what is known as **Ye Fountain of Perpetual Mirth**. The width of the fountain's stone base is roughly 20 feet in length. Frank Crisp surrounded it with four mermaids that are dressed as Nuns. Above them are four Dolphins with Friars' heads. In the basin are

Ye Terrace Garden

water lilies of various colors. It is filled with gold fish. Looking around you, there are bunches of statues of storks. There are two large Japanese storks with babies in their mouths. There are eight smaller Japanese storks with stones that are placed at different points of the garden. The Visitors' Guide mentions that:

According to the Danish story a stork is supposed to come to a house with the birth of each addition to the family. Stones are also seen in the birds' mouths, in accordance with the belief that they bore stones with them when they were migrating, in order that they might not be swept out of their course by the wind. Or, as another version has it, that they might not make a noise; and bring the eagles and other birds of prey upon themselves. A sentinel stork also held a stone in one claw to keep awake while the others slept.

Directly in the middle of the fountain are two sets of stairs that flair out in different directions, on to a path referred to as **Ye pathe of joye by whyche ye wanderer can go anyways.**

Soon after purchasing Friar Park, George Harrison placed a Hindu statue in the center of the fountain and placed colorful garden gnomes around the perimeter. He later immortalized **Ye Fountain of Perpetual Mirth** in the lyrics to his song, *The Ballad of Sir Frankie Crisp*.

Ye Pathe of Joye by whyche ye wanderer can go anyways

You were just standing next to Ye Fountain of Perptual Mirth at the edge of the Terrace Garden on the east side of the House. You have descended a staircase before you that leads to a foot path that the Visitors' Guide refers to as:

"Ye path of joye by whyche ye wanderer can go anyways."

You are rather high up on the end of the descending plateau and there are trees on your left and to the right is a wide and long stretch of lawn. Further down there is a large expanse of water about half way to the end of the property. It seems to be about 150 feet in width and nearly 300 feet in length. Large rocks can be seen along the edges of the lake. At the far end is a long red bow-shaped bridge that crosses from one inlet to another. In the distance beyond that you can see tree-filled hills about a mile away on the other side of the river. The lake is surrounded by trees on every side including blue spruce, California Pines, and Weeping Willows. There are even some planted on a small island that can be seen at the far end. In the foreground, about 50 feet from the water's edge, closest to where you are standing, you can see three people – two women and a man - walking along the left sides of the lake. They seem to be looking in, and admiring . . . something. Perhaps some fish? Perhaps some water lilies? Perhaps some sculptures? From this far away it simply is not possible to know. But then the man in the party begins to slowly, and ever-so-carefully, put one leg in front of the other, and then he seems to step into the water. That seems odd. He is fully dressed, in creased trousers and a jacket that seems to be made of sturdy tweed. In fact, he still has his hat on. He then follows with the other leg and continues forward into the water. He seems to be about chest high at this point. Now he stops. He turns to the ladies in his party and motions for them to follow him.

The one with the dark hair is wearing a tweed suit. Her mass of wavy hair has been swept up to the top of her head and is gathered into a knot. The one with the lighter hair is wearing an ankle-length skirt with a matching jacket. She is wearing a huge, broad-brimmed hat that is decorated with a pink ribbon. They look at one another, and then at him, and then at one another again, and then the one in the dress walks right into the water! Seconds later her friend follows! They are now in the water. And they are laughing!

The gal in the hat walks forward and then backwards a few steps. You watch as they continue walking toward the other side of the lake with most of their bodies fully submerged. They do it so quickly and easily and gracefully, too. Moments pass and they begin to emerge. One by one. But strangely enough, they have not gotten wet at all. This is clearly another one of Frank Crisp's unusual optical illusions. This is quite a mystery. How did three people walk into the lake, cross over completely, and emerge without a drop of water on them? The lake seems to be at least 200 feet away. At this point you have had a far-off view of the lake. Now it is time for you to investigate and find out just how they did that. To do so will require you to get a closer view of the lake at Friar Park.

Ye Stepping Stones whyche offer ye safe passage & grand illusions

You are continuing to descend down the lawn roughly 200 ft. as much of the land slopes down around you on both sides. There are trees planted to the left and there is an area of trees in front of you with a domed, round shelter on the edge. As you get closer you see that it is an authentic Native American wigwam. You keep walking further down the grassy field until you reach the edge of the lake.

From far back on the Terrace Garden this looked like one large expanse of water but now that you are closer you see that you have fallen for another one of Frank Crisp's illusions! This is not one large pool of water after all. There are actually two pools of water, arranged in tiers, with water flowing down from the highest, down to the lowest. There are a series of stepping stones in this upper level, but they are at water level so clearly those people are not walking on those. Otherwise it would have merely looked as if they were walking on water and not through it. So you'll have to go down a bit - about 50 ft. further - to figure that one out, but while you are here at the water's edge perhaps it might be interesting to walk across these stepping stones. The length and width of the lake at

this point is roughly 50 ft. The stepping stones are large enough to accommodate both your feet at the same time, with room to spare. They are in an assortment of shapes and sizes. They look heavy but yet they seem to be floating on the surface of the water. So you put your foot forward and step on to the first stone. Everything seems fine so you go to the next one. Then you take another step. You are now surrounded by water on every side. You can see fish swimming below the shimmering surface. Another step and you are now half way there. Stop for a moment. Enjoy the view around you. To your left is the lake, to your right is the small pool of water, and then the grassy lawn leading up toward the house. There are people at the terrace, up by the house. They are pointing at you. To them, right now, you appear to be walking on the water! You reach an inlet that you are able to walk upon with more stepping stones that you follow down toward the edge of the small pool. You now pass a gold-fish pond. Next to it there is a sign that says:

"HERONS WILL BE PROSECUTED"

As you continue walking you can hear the sound of water falling. When you look to your left you see that there is indeed an actual waterfall. It is located on the edge of the second tier. It is here where the water falls off of a shelf and down into the larger body of water. But that is not the biggest surprise. You are standing on the spot where the man and women emerged from the lake after having crossed over. It is now that you see how you had been fooled. You see, they never touched a drop of water. To your left is the waterfall. To your right is the lower lake. Right in front of you are a series of very large, and varied stepping stones like the ones you just crossed. It is because they are so low, and that the upper tier of the

Ye Stepping Stones

pool is so high, that from the terrace garden and house it looked like they were walking *through* the water. But they were simply walking *across* the stepping stones! What an amazing illusion. If you look to your left you can see that more people have gathered up on the terrace garden. Many are looking down here. Now its your turn to cross over. The distance is a bit further since the lake is wider here. It's about 65 ft. in length. So you take your first step, and then another, and then another, and then another. There are roughly 20 stepping stones and you are half way across right now.

What an astounding mind the great Frank Crisp has, to encourage something like this being built on his grand property. Wait. What is this? The Stepping Stones have impressions of the bare feet of a man. There are also some that are narrow. Clearly they are meant to be a woman's feet. And then there are several smaller and narrower impressions which are likely those from the bare feet of children. A bit further away are the footprints of a four-footed animal with claws. Now look. The footprints of the man have turned around to face the claw prints of the beast. The footprints of the female and children do not continue to the end of the lake. You know what? This seems to be some sort of puzzle for you to solve. What could all this mean? It seems to me that the man turned around to fight off the beast and was likely eaten! And the reason why the other footprints disappeared can't be too easily explained. Perhaps at that point, to escape the beast, they jumped into the lake? But who knows? Isn' it amazing how surprises and stories and puzzles and illusions await you everywhere you go in Friar Park? You now walk up the stone steps, and the people above see that you are completely dry. No doubt they are quite amazed, and as confused as you were, as they see you walking out of the lake, completely dry.

As you leave the lake, here is some cool trivia you might like to know: This is an artificial lake. Everything about it is man-made. Even the rocks around them, and the stepping stones, were created with Pulhamite, which was a material invented, patented, and manufactured by James Pulham and Son. They were a well-known firm of Victorian landscape gardeners and terracotta manufacturers. They also made garden ornaments. The firm was best known for the construction of rock gardens, follies and grottoes in which the firm used both natural stone and their own invention. Pulhamite, which usually looked like gritty sandstone, was used to join natural rocks together or crafted to simulate natural stone features. The recipe to create Pulhamite went to the grave with him. When Frank Crisp purchased this grand property in the 1800s, there was already a house in this location that Mr. Frank Crisp had torn down. That house even once had its own approach driveway, as did the other that was once on there. When George Harrison first acquired the magical and magnificent property the lakes were filled with layers of rubbish. There are alternative stories to why this was the case. One is that the nuns could not afford the upkeep so they allowed the lakes to be used as a dumping ground. The other story is that the lakes were drained and filled in for the benefit of the students who attended the school in the 1950s and 1960s.

Either way, when George Harrison acquired the property he and some of the male Hare Krishna Devotees who he invited to live at Friar Park took on the task of clearing out the lakes with the assistance of some WWII-era flame throwers. It took 4.5 years to renovate the lakes.

Who would have guessed such amazing stories could be found in the simple creation of an artificial lake?

Ye Japanese Garden

There comes upon you the year 1910. The month is June. You have been spending the day at Friar Park. You have just walked back cross the water-level stepping stones and are now following the stepping stones on the ground, through a grassy area along a well-travelled foot path. There are trees to your right which block your view of the house. To your left are small trees and a series of man-made hills that conceal what is on the other side. After a few moments you reach a cross-road that gives you the opportunity to turn left or right. You turn left and now the man-made hills are to your left, along with a row of trees. To the right you see that the lake has narrowed to a small inlet. There are stepping stones along each side.

You now get a frontal view of the **Tea House**, on an elevated hill, with a waterfall in front of it, in the center of the garden that you saw when you first entered Friar Park. You cross over a wood bow bridge that spans a narrow inlet. Now you are back on the path, and then you cross over another bow bridge. Though this time there is not an inlet, but it seems as if there is a stream to your left and the water from it drains into the portion of the pond to your right which is much more expansive at this point. The path begins turning to your left and you continue following it until there is a fork in the road. From here you see straight ahead another large pool of water. This is very inviting.

To your right is a beautiful **Stone Bridge** and beyond that is a red bow bridge that spans an inlet, and there are also a series of flat plank bridges to be able to traverse the other two inlets on the right side of this large pool. You turn left and walk up a winding path that has trees to your left and right. Like elsewhere in Friar Park these trees seem perfectly placed in order to help postpone any reveal of what lies ahead.

Thereby leaving visitors like you to be astonished at what you see when it comes into full view. And that certainly is the case here as you enter this valley. On the right is a Japanese structure with a domed roof.

To your left is a stream that leads to the bow bridge you crossed over, and as you take a few steps further in you finally see where you are. You have found yourself right in the middle of **Ye Japanese Garden**! Yes. A Japanese garden. Right here in early twentieth century England. No one could possibly have expected to see this.

There is much to learn about Japanese Gardens. Not just their design and construction, but about how they affect visitors. It has been said that *"unless a garden has an air of peace it's not a place worth visiting. It should be a place where the mind finds rest and relaxation."* That is certainly the case here.

Based on information in the Visitors Guide, Frank Crisp revealed that Friar Park's Japanese Garden was inspired by an illustration by Josiah Conder from his 1893 book "Landscape Gardening in Japan." So all of this was created by studying, and trying to recreate, what was seen only in an illustration. This is truly incredible.

You are standing at the entry and you see that it has incorporated numerous oriental elements. Directly in front of you are paths of stepping stones that you can follow in an assortment of directions. There is a pond in the center that is encircled with large stones. If you go straight it will lead you to a boarded bridge that goes to a small island made of dirt and stones in the middle of it. There is only room for a

Ye Japanese Garden

Japanese lantern on it, and a Japanese Maple tree, and some stepping stones. The stone lantern on the island has four legs and a very wide umbrella-shaped cap. It is called a "**snow-scene lantern**" because the broad surface is designed in such a way that snow can rest upon it. You then cross a stone bridge on the right to get off the island and then follow a path that leads to a series of man-made hills. Along the way there are more lanterns, stones, and trees. There is even a water well in the distance. Directly in front of you, on the other side of the pond, is a waterfall. If you follow the path straight to your left you will pass a bamboo fence. You will then pass a tall and thin, ornamental stone lantern consisting of an earth ring base, a pedestal, and then a central platform that holds a hexagonal-shaped fire box beneath a small stone umbrella with 6 sides, and a rounded-jewel top.

    The path then continues along the side of the pond until you cross over an arched wood bridge with short posts & double rails. You are now on a path that is surrounded with Japanese plants that leads to a bright red, wood tea house next to the hill on that side. Over there are golden-yellow clipped Yews. It is interesting to note that, though candles can be placed inside some of the lanterns, they are not meant for illumination at night. The best they could do is to offer some dim and mysterious light, but not much more. Instead, they are placed here to be strictly ornamental. Evergreen Conifers have been planted over there. Far to your right is a large stone lantern with a Wisteria growing alongside of it by the waterside. Directly to your left is a stone lantern and a multi-tiered pagoda. Over there are Japanese Maples in shades of crimson and purple. Near the Stone Bridge is a granite lantern on a curved stem above a heavy square base. It adds a beautiful focal point while easily blending into the natural landscape.

    In the Visitors Guide Frank Crisp shared a story that there is a prevalent opinion that the Japanese Gardens of England do not in any way resemble the Japanese Gardens of Japan. To illustrate this, he mentions the legendary tale of a well-known horticulturist who created a Japanese Garden on his property. Upon completion, he invited a Japanese gentleman of his acquaintance to inspect it and give an opinion upon it. The Japanese gentleman was full of admiration but had failed to recognize that it was intended for a true landscape garden of his own country. Wishing to be extra polite he said, "It is very beautiful. We have nothing like it in Japan." As a result, Frank Crisp decided that his Japanese Garden should be based upon an undoubted Japanese precedent. That is why he emulated the illustration from Conder's book, since he was England's foremost expert on Japanese gardens. So, comparing that 1893 illustration to the design of this Japanese garden, you can deduce the following:

There are five hills in this garden. **Hill #1** has broad, sweeping sides. It has a pathway near its base, and the cascading waterfall has been arranged just in front of it. The others are somewhat lower and seem to be of secondary importance. **Hill #2** is somewhat lower and also of secondary importance. **Hill #3** is more like a lateral ridge and is a sort of sub peak. **Hill #4** is in the foreground, to the left of the pond. It is small, low, and rounded. **Hill #5** is steep in form and partially hidden below, with little or no detail upon it, as it is meant to represent a distant peak in mountain scenery.

Then there are the trees. Seven of them have symbolic meaning and importance to the design of this garden. **Tree #1** is located at the central part of the background. It represents the **"Tree of Upright Spirit."** **Tree #2** is planted in the foreground of the island. It is called the **"View-perfecting Tree."** **Tree #3** is the **"Tree of Solitude."** It is actually not one tree at all, but is a group of trees with thick foliage in the background on the far left side. **Tree #4** is planted at the side of the waterfall, to hide a portion of it. This tree is called the **"Cascade-Screening Tree."** **Tree #5** is the **"Tree of the Setting Sun."** It is typically planted on the west side of the garden in order to filter the glare of the setting sun. **Tree #6** is called the **"Distancing Pine."** The idea of planting these pines is to suggest a far-off forest. It is therefore placed behind the further hills of the garden and partly hidden from view. **Tree #7** leans over the lake, with its branches sprawling over the water. This tree is located in the foreground, to your right, near the bridge crossing the island in the pond.

While there are plenty of stones throughout the garden, around the pond, and along the paths, there are also specifically chosen and placed in various parts of the garden that are significant in telling a visual story, and are arranged to produce harmony. The most important of these is referred to as the **"Guardian Stone."** It is the heart of the garden, and is considered to be the garden's center. In this garden it's placed high, and in an upright position, and forms the flank of the cliff over which the cascade of the waterfall pours into the pond. A companion to that stone, located on the opposite side of the waterfall, at a lower altitude, is referred to as the **"Cliff Stone."** It is identified by its flat top, and it arches over slightly so as to screen a portion of the torrent. Then comes the **"Worshipping Stone."** It is located on the island in the lake. It is a broad and flat, and indicates the central position for worshipping gods. That is why it is typically in an open space that is

Ye Japanese Garden

accessible by stepping stones.

To your right, in an island on a small lagoon next to you, is what is called the **"Perfect View Stone."** It is always located on the side of the garden and in the nearer foreground, to maintain its true prominence in the landscape. Somewhat similar in shape, and located at the edge of the pond, on the left-hand side, and rising high above the water's surface, is what is known as the **"Waiting Stone."** The sixth stone that has symbolic meaning in a Japanese garden is known as the **"Moon Shadow Stone."** It occupies an important position in the distance. It is located in a hollow between the two principal hills and in front of the distant peak. And then there is Stone #7, which is way in the back.

You cross over the wood plank bridge in front of you, and you stop for a moment to take in the surroundings, and listen to the sounds of the waterfall. You cross over the island, and then over the stone bridge, and turn left. You walk toward the back of the garden, and keep walking, until you are in close proximity to the erect **"Cave Stone."** It is easily spotted because it is located beside the central trees, and two broad, flat rocks are placed with it. Turning around, you get a grand view of the Japanese garden from the northwest corner. You are surrounded by natural and man-made features that are meant to be symbolic and to have various meanings to those walking through this Japanese garden.

Over there, you can see a pine tree that is being trained to look twisted and bent, as if it was done by the elements to represent, and to be a metaphor for, the aged individual who has stood the tests of time and fate.

Walking back, to your left, beneath the **Tree of the Setting Sun**, you can see the **"Seat of Honor Stone."** It is a broad, flat stone, and has been placed in a horizontal position. So, now that you have an idea of the design of the garden around you, let's return to where you started. You cross over the stone bridge, step upon the island, and once again you take a moment to enjoy the surroundings, and to listen to the wonderful and calming sounds of the waterfall. The sound of the rapidly running water from the cascade adds to the soothing nature of the garden.

You recall George Harrison once saying that looking at, and listening to, water is beneficial, and that it soothes one's nerves. Some may say it soothes one's soul. It adds balance to the garden and it adds balance to one's life. What Frank Crisp has done here is beyond price. In fact, it is beyond measure.

You cross back over the wood-boarded bridge and follow the stepping stones and are now back where you started. That brings you to the stone that is right beneath your feet. At this point you couldn't possibly get any closer to it. The stone right there is called the **"Pedestal Stone."** It occupies the first rank among the stepping stones arranged in the foreground of the garden, and is at the parting of the various directions. From this stone you can turn in any direction and follow more stepping stones.

The tenth most significant and symbolic stone in the garden is known as the **"Idling Stone."** Though that is singular, it actually consists of a pair of broad, low, and slightly rounded stones. They are always placed near the edge of the water, in some shade, and in the mid-distance of the garden. From here, you see that it is directly behind the island, and to the right of the cascade. It certainly gives character to the edge of the water.

The sun is burning bright above you now. Let's find a way to cool off a bit, shall we? Walking straight, you come across a date-shaped stone that has a round water basin at the top. This one is set on a base and is elevated enough so that one can easily wash one's hands. So go ahead. Dip your hands into it. Move your fingers around. How does the water feel? Go ahead and splash some water on to your face. Can you feel the cool droplets as they rapidly run down your forehead, and cheeks, and chin. Now splash some ontothe back of your neck.

Can you feel the cool droplets as they rapidly run down the center and sides of your back, toward your waist? Doesn't that feel great? Want to drink some of the cool water? Go ahead. It's just rainwater that has collected in the basin. Lean forward and cup some water into your hands.

Ye Japanese Garden

Can you feel the fresh, cool rainwater swishing within the inside of your mouth, and upon your tongue, and then down your throat as you swallow?

Look over there. It is a wood-walled tea house.

There is a breeze rushing in from in front of you, and you smell the pleasing perfume of the freshly unfurled flowers. But looking around you see that there are no flowers around you. So the scent must be coming from elsewhere. As Frank Crisp pointed out in his Visitor's Guide:

Japanese Gardens are not flower gardens. To many it seems impossible that a garden without flowers could be a thing of beauty. As it may appear to Western ideas, flowers for their own sake do not enter into the scheme of Japanese gardening. The gardener in Japan is not a cultivator of flowers, but a Garden Artist.

And Frank Crisp is certainly correct on that one, as he seems to be correct on all things. But, though there are no flowers, there most certainly are shrubs and plants, many of which may flower. The ones around you include a selection of **Almond** trees. There are brightly blooming **Cherry Blossom** trees. The **Plum** trees are a fine addition since they still bloom even if there is snow on the ground. Ah! Perhaps it is the sweet-smelling fragrance of the **Wistaria** trees that is perfuming the garden. The one over there is in a relatively open area, so it can receive plenty of sunlight, and it has alluring lavender blooms.

The evergreen **Camellia**, that now has white flowers, guarantees continual color in the garden throughout the winter. Of course the real reason it is here is likely because tea is made from its leaves. And of course this Japanese garden would not be complete without **Maples** of various kinds. They always add grace and beauty throughout the seasons.

Just looking in any direction, you can see them - some are 8 feet tall and wide - with their deeply cut, feathery leaves, some red, some red-purple, some bright crimson, others pink-tinged, and more. There is even a diversity of dwarf **Japanese Maples**. Some have delicately weeping habits, while others form a flowing mound of foliage. There is also an assembly of dwarfed **Pine**, and cranes formed of **Larch**. There is also a **Japanese Medlar** - the evergreen that offers pear-shaped fruit that has grown in Japan for the past 1,000 years.

The Japanese garden is absolutely and incredibly lovely, but neither I, nor Frank Crisp can possibly describe any of this as well as Milton's words in Paradise Lost, which are as follows:

" . . . the crisped brooks,
Rowling on Oriental Pearl and sands of gold,
With mazy error under pendant shades,
Ran nectar, visiting each plant, and fed
Flowers worthy of Paradise."

You have just visited the **Japanese Garden**, that is located to the south of the lakes on the southeast side of the property. Now prepare yourself to see much more as you continue your grand tour of Friar Park.

Below: The original reference illustration used to design the Japanese garden. Hills - 1, Near Mountain; 2, Companion Mountain; 3, Mountain Spur; 4, Near Hill; 5, Distant Peak. Stones - 1, Guardian Stone; 2, Cliff Stone; 3, Worshipping Stone, 4, Perfect View Stone; 5, Waiting Stone; 6, Moon Shadow Stone; 7, Cave, or Kwannon Stone; 8, Seat of Honor Stone; 9, Pedestal Stone. Trees - 1, Principal Tree; 2, View-Perfecting Tree; 3, Tree of Solitude; 4, Cascade-Screening Tree; 5, Tree of the Setting Stone; 6, Distant Pine; 7, Stretching Pine. A, Garden Well; B, Stone-View Lantern; C, Garden Gate; D, Boarding Bridge; E, Plank Bridge; F, Stone Bridge; G, Water Basin; I, Garden Shrine.

Rowing upon ye North & South Poole

You are seated in a row boat in the northern portion of Friar Park's lake. Along the perimeter are man-made stones that have been so authentically sculpted and colored that they really are indistinguishable from real rocks. Looking all around, you see a Weeping Willow, a Blue Spruce, numerous Pines trees, a Golden Yew, a 100 ft. tall Tasmanian Blue Gum, and a variety of other beautiful trees. Ornamental grasses have also been lavishly planted and give bright colors and dazzling views around the lake throughout the year. On the east side are mass plantings of an assortment of bamboos. There are also numerous prehistoric-looking greenery plants called Gunnera. They are sometimes called Dinosaur Food. Their deeply-lobed leaves can get up to 4 feet across and the plant can stand up to 8 ft. tall. They are clearly thriving in the boggy ground that was created on the edge of the lake.

Being in the boat gives you an idea of how low you are in this basin. The ground around the lake ascends in every direction. From here you can take in an outstanding view of the magnificent house upon the hill, across the sweeping green lawn. The morning sunlight is gleaming upon the bricks, the red clay tiles, the light stone, the pinnacles, and the finials atop the roof.

Looking around at eye level, you see the stepping stones and water falling off the shelf of the upper tier of the lake. Since you are rowing you pick up the pace with the oars and begin to row the boat under the

Rowing upon ye North & South Poole

stone bridge. The stone bridge is about 15 ft. -16 ft. across, and only about 6 ft. above the surface of the water, but being seated in this boat, you can row beneath without having to duck your head. And there it is above your head. It is not a wide bridge, just meant for people to cross over from one path to another.

The lake at Friar Park is an artificial lake. Everything about it is man-made. Even the rocks around them, and the stepping stones were created with Pulhamite, which is a material invented, patented, and manufactured by James Pulham and Son. They are a firm of Victorian landscape gardeners and terracotta manufacturers. They also make garden ornaments. The firm is best known for the construction of rock gardens, follies and grottoes in which the firm used both natural stone and their own invention. Pulhamite, which usually looks like gritty sandstone, is used to join natural rocks together or crafted to simulate natural stone features.

You are now in the lower portion of the lake, known as the South Poole. Up above you can see and hear blissful birds circling in the distance. A half dozen delightful ducks are gliding effortlessly along the surface of the water. All around you are jubilant displays of wide brimmed and chromatic lilies gently floating in place. Looking down upon the clear surface you see reflections of billowy white clouds in the sky. Focusing down around the boat you see an assortment of multicolored and vibrant fish swimming beneath the surface.

Up ahead on the western edge of the lake you see the opening of a cave that seems to be made of rough, natural-looking stone. Because there is grass along the top and the sides, the entry to this cave could not be seen from above, or from the paths around it. It is perhaps roughly 5 ft. in width and height. Throughout past centuries, and in countless stories, caves have been known to be the homes of gnomes, and spirits, and dragons, and monsters and even treasures. The great mythologist Joseph Campbell has said that **"The cave you fear to enter holds the treasure you seek."**

What do you think is the purpose of this cave? Perhaps this is a place where Frank Crisp hosts initiations and ceremonies. As you likely know, in Plato's "Allegory of the Cave," he described a gathering of people who spent their lives living in cave, chained to a wall, watching shadows go by. They refused to try to escape & venture to the outside world and did not want to know or hear of what might be out there. They just wanted to stick to living in the shadows and know of nothing else. So, what you want to do? Here you are, in the comfort of the boat, on this lovely lake, under the bright sunlight, and you are relaxed, and there is no stress, and no anxiety, and all is well.

How eager are you to take on a challenge? Do you think you are ready to leave the light, and all that you can see, and all that you know, and enter a place where mystery - and perhaps even danger - awaits? Take some time to think about it. There is no rush to decide. There is never a rush to do anything on a day like this. So for now just sit back, take in the views, watch the fish swim below, and delight in the ducks gliding by, and observe the birds above, and tune in to the trees as they sway in the breeze, as you joyfully row in a boat in the southern portion of the lake at Friar Park.

Ye Brydge of Stone to traverse ye Pooles

You are on a gravel footpath with the Japanese Garden to your left and the southern portion of the lake to your right. The northern portion is in front of you. As the path curves right you have the option of stepping off this path now to follow a series of stepping stones leading down or you can walk onto the arched stone bridge ahead. This stone bridge crosses over the narrowest portion of the lake which is roughly 15 ft. - 16 ft. in width. At its widest points the upper portion is roughly 250 ft. across and the lower portion is roughly 350 ft. across. So this area that connects the two is clearly the best for the placement of a stone bridge. The bridge looks weather-worn with some of the color of the wide slabs being washed away. Some areas having portions that are black, and beige, and brown, and dirty white. There are even some areas that are greenish, no doubt from the growth of moss along the sides of the stone slabs. The bridge looks like it has been here for 500 years. That is a strong-looking bridge. No fear of crumbling. The base stones seem to be set into the bedrock on each side. This being done in order for it to resist any shifting or any sideways movement of the stones from its own weight, or that of any pedestrian traffic along its top.

Interestingly, from this perspective, it certainly does not appear to be a horizontal bridge that is held up by an arch made out of flatish - though slightly trapezoidal-shaped - stones and mortar. Instead the entire bridge itself forms an arch with the use of well-cut, strong stones, and some sort

Above: View of the stone bridge from the northwest.

of mortar, giving it the strength to connect to land on the other side. The water from the two pools seamlessly connect and flow below it. The beautiful arched bridge over water creates a perfectly symmetrical reflection. The bridge seems like the best route to take, so off you go.

Take a look over there. You can see a bathing place for birds off the path on the other side. You stop and take in the view around you. The northernmost edge of the lake is roughly 220 feet from the bridge you are on. Looking south east, you take in a beautiful view of the sloping valley that contains the Alpine Meadow. On the right side of the pool are a series of stepping stones that lead to a red lacquered spanning bridge that arches gracefully over a small lagoon. The design was inspired by the Sacred Bridge of Nikko which is considered to be one of the most beautiful structures in the Empire of Japan. On the other side of the red bridge is a bit of land with some stepping stones that then lead to a bamboo plank bridge in a zig-zag that crosses over another lagoon. Legend says that the design of bamboo zig-zag bridges is meant to fool bad spirits.

Along the right side of that inlet of land between the two bridges is a garden dedicated to the Greek Goddess of the Rainbow. It is an Iris Garden that is worthy of Mount Olympus. The area is blooming lavishly with flowering plants that have long, erect stems with shiny flowers, in luscious colors of purple, pink, and endless bicolors. There are also groups of yellow, blue, white, and red Iris flowers. In 1899, the following

Ye Brydge of Stone

was written about that which is before you:

Presently the bog-garden comes into view, here Irises and other semi-aquatic species of plants and Ferns have been planted, but this feature will be largely extended. The bog-garden adjoins the lake, a pretty piece of water, containing an island that adds very considerably to the charms of the scene. The outlines of island and lake are informal, and the planting that has been done accentuates the points of beauty.

Floating along in beatific bliss and glorious glee are a handful of Straight-of-Magellan Geese. The males have a white head and breast, whereas the females are brown with black-striped wings and yellow feet. Over there are a bunch of Rosybill Ducks. It is easy to spot them thanks to the distinctive red bill on males and the slate-colored bill on females. There are also some Shoveller Ducks swimming right below the bridge right now. Each has a large spatulate bill.

The breeding drake has an iridescent dark green head, white breast and chestnut belly and flanks. The female is a drab, blotched brown like other dabblers, but easily distinguished by the long broad bill which is gray and tinged with orange on the cutting edge and lower jaw. The female's forewing is gray.

The Spoonbill Ducks can be spotted from very far away thanks to its large spoon-shaped bill which widens towards the tip and creates a unique shape. The males have an iridescent green head and neck, white chest and breast and chestnut belly and sides. The females have a light brownish head with a blackish crown and a brownish speckled body. Their bill is olive green with fleshy orange in the gape area and speckled with black dots. Mandarin Ducks are also in the ponds. The adult male is a striking and unmistakable bird. It has a red bill, a large white crescent above the eye, and a reddish face and "whiskers". The female is similar to the female wood duck, with a white eye-ring and stripe running back from the eye, but is paler below, has a small white flank stripe, and a pale tip to its bill.  Over there are some Tufted Ducks. The adult male is all black except for white flanks and a blue-grey bill with gold-yellow eyes. There is a tuft on its head. The adult female is brown with paler flanks, and is more easily confused with other diving ducks.

Carolina Ducks are over there, with their distinctive multicolored iridescent plumage and red eyes, with a distinctive white flare down the neck. The female, less colorful, has a white eye-ring and a whitish throat. Both adults have crested heads. And then there are the Japanese Teal Ducks. From this distance, the drakes plumage appear grey, with a dark head, a yellowish behind, and a white stripe running along the flanks. Their head and upper neck is chestnut, with a wide and iridescent dark green patch of half-moon or teardrop-shape that starts immediately before the eye and arcs to the upper hind-neck.

There is so much to see around the south and east and north sides of this large pool of water, as well as that which is on and in the water, including plenty of gold fish, turtles swimming about beneath the water's surface. Looking down to your right, there is a shallow inlet where a small row boat is tied up against a wood post.

At this point, it may be a good idea to take a mental break from all these fantastic surprises that seem to await you around every corner in Friar Park.

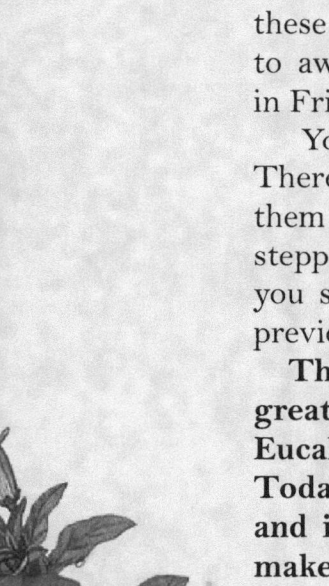

You cross the bridge and follow the path downhill. There is a bench to your right where two people are seated. You smile at them and the man tips his hat as you turn left and follow along down the stepping stones that lead to the shiny red bridge. But before you get to it you stop in order to untie the rope. The circa 1899 article mentioned previously described what is to your right as follows:

The Bamboos will be very appropriate when they have grown to a greater size, and in a sheltered situation a group of plants of Eucalyptus globulus have been unharmed during three winters. Today the lake is a conspicuous and effective feature of the gardens, and it takes one by surprise to be told that it is quite of artificial make, and that upon the same site was once a private residence. The change has been brought about by the well-known firm of Messrs. Pulham & Son, of Broxbourne, who are responsible for several very artistic pieces of work at Friar Park, both with the famous Pulhamite, and in other matters relating to water and rock work.

The boat is now aligned along the water's edge. Are you ready? And the boat is off and out . . .

You have just visited the Stone Bridge that is located in the middle of the lake located on the southeast portion of the property. Now take a good look around because there is so much more to see.

Since you are already in the boat, it would make sense to continue on exploring the lake, to see what other surprises await you in this portion of Friar Park.

Entrance & journey through ye Water Caves

You have been spending quite a bit of time in a row boat, floating leisurely upon the lake, and now it is time to decide about whether or not to row into the entry to the cave to see what is inside. Remember, once inside, you won't be able to change your mind. After all, the entry is low and narrow, and dark. Once you enter it does not seem possible to easily turn round.

This is a unique opportunity. After a brief moment, you row away from the edge and you are soon in the center of the south portion of the lake. You are getting closer and closer to the entry to the cave.

Are you ready? If so, then take in a deep breath and close your eyes for a quick second to prepare yourself. Now open your eyes wide. This is it. The point of no return. You can do this. So, you begin to row & you row & you row & then you pull in the oars.

You now float through the opening as the daylight behind you disappears. It is suddenly very quiet. And dark. It is pitch black. You can not see the walls. You have left the real world behind. What awaits you up ahead, in the darkness? Nothing is ever as it seems here at Friar Park. You have entered an underworld. Situations like this are not always pleasant ones. To quote HOMER:

"Lest for my daring Persephone the dread,
From Hades should send up an awful monster's grisly head."

That gives you no comfort whatsoever. Does Medusa lurk in the shadows around the bend, with the venomous snakes upon her head, waiting to strike at you? If so, then be prepared. The slightest gaze upon her face turns any living thing to stone.

You slowly put the oars back in the water, careful not to hit the sides of the cave. They sink down below the surface and you slowly begin to row forward, bracing yourself for whatever awaits you ahead.

Now look up. There is some blue light in the near distance. You row along a very dark passage and then around a corner. There is some blue light ahead and then . . . you are now *immersed* in the blue light. Looking around you see that you have entered an enormous cave that is shimmering with a beautiful blue hue. But where is the light coming from? Look up. The luminescence is the result of prismatic panes of glass that are strategically placed in the ground over the top of the cave. This creates a brilliant blue reflection that illuminates the cavern.

To many visitors, this cave may look familiar. That is because it is a replica of the Blue Grotto on the island of Capri, off of southern Italy.

This is stunning. It does not seem possible.

You are underground, beneath the Japanese garden at Friar Park, in an incredible and large cave, and you are immersed in sunlight that has been transformed to blue light. Could this be a dream?

You slowly and carefully place your hand over the boat and into the water. It feels chilled, but not cold. So you just bring your hand back in, and keep rowing forward, to see were this leads you next.

You are now reaching the end of this large blue cave and you are now entering a narrow passage.

It is getting dark again. Along the sides of the caves are stone and terracotta statues of Swans & White Owls.

This portion of the water cave has electric illuminations to keep it from being too dark. The cave is now getting narrower and darker, and then begins to widen. Along the sides are stone statues of **Bats, Frogs, and Toadstools.** Or are they even stone statues at all? Perhaps they were the sad, unfortunate victims of

Medusa's deadly glares? To your left and right you see **Fossil Trees** and even some petrified bird's nests that are also made of stone. And in the water are crocodiles, but don't be scared. They are just models of crocodiles with eyes that are lit up with electric lamps.

Suddenly, you can hear the sounds of rushing water, and the sound is getting louder . . . and louder . . . and louder, and you are paddling a bit faster . . . and faster . . . and faster . . . and there is some light up ahead.

You are clearly directly beneath the top portion of the lake because, to your right, you can see that light is entering through the pillars of the overflowing curtain of water. Light is bouncing off the stucco walls of the tunnel. It can not possibly get more magical than this.

Somehow, someway, Frank Crisp had arranged for electricity to run through the cave! You can see numerous gnomes, in various positions, along the side walls of the cave. It is impossible to imagine how they are doing this but they have managed to use electric lighting to create an underground rainbow! Wow. You are in wonderland. You really & truly are.

As you leave the roar of the waterfall and the sunlight behind you are soon paddling, once again, through the pitch-black. There are some more electric illuminations up ahead. Now here is something even more interesting. There is a platform along the perimeter of a portion of the cave, and you see people are walking alongside of it. So clearly rowing a boat is not the only way to enjoy the beauty of these underwater caves, so you continue rowing . . . and rowing . . . and rowing.

You continue rowing through the darkness until you finally see a ray of light in the distance. You begin to paddle slower because you do not want this experience to end. But you have enjoyed this unique experience so much, and others are likely waiting for the opportunity to make use of this boat for their own underland wonderland adventure.

The exit is getting closer . . . and closer . . . and . . . closer, and like the entry, it is about five feet in width and height.

And   now   you   are   out.

Yes. You are now back in the daylight. You can feel the warm sunshine upon your head and face and arms and hands. It sure feels wonderful. Look around. Where are you? Ah ha! You have found yourself in a small inlet in the northwest regions of the northern portion of the lake. So you row to the edge of the lake. There are some ropes to your left. So you tie the boat up and step out of it ever so carefully. Take it slow. You need to get your bearings and remind yourself that you are back in the real world. In the distance, on the green lawn, perhaps 25 feet from the lake's edge, you see three ladies and two gentleman huddled together. When one of the ladies moves slightly to the left you see that they are talking to a gentleman who looks just like George Harrison. He averts his attention from them for a brief moment and looks at you. He is bathed in golden sunlight, some of which reflect off of his eyes, making them seem to sparkle. He slightly nods in acknowledgment that you have made it out of the caves. In a flash, he is hidden from view again. Was he really there at all? Perhaps you'll never know. You take a look round and you see that there is a large Chestnut Tree with a bed of Winter-Aconite underneath, displaying its yellow, cup-shaped flowers. As you approach it you are reminded of the old Chinese proverb that says:

> **"The one who plants the tree
> is not the one who will enjoy its shade."**

You see small trees around the area that Frank Crisp and his gardener Philip Knowles and their team of gardeners have planted. They both knew that it would be many years - many decades, in fact - before anyone would enjoy their shade. They were visionaries. They designed how Friar Park would look in the future, even though they would not be the ones here to fully enjoy all they were doing.

The cascade of water that you rowed past while underground can be heard behind you. You look and see the row of stepping stones that completely span the width of the pool. You take in a deep breath, and close your eyes. Now open them. Everything is still here. Just as it was before you went into the cave. Everything was real. Nothing has changed. But yet, somehow, you feel as if you have changed. You went into the darkness and conquered any fears you may have had of what may have waited for you inside. And like all heroes who emerge from the darkness, you are returning with a renewed sense of what is possible, and what you and others can accomplish if one is willing to take a leap into the unknown and continue upon a quest. You took on a challenge, and you followed through until the end.

Your time at Friar Park is shaping your personality by putting some unforeseen challenges before you. Your time at Friar Park is making you a better person.

Look! There is a tall white tent set up at the water's edge. Perhaps it might make sense to sit there for awhile and reflect on what you have just experienced, and perhaps relive it a bit. Because it was quite unlike anything you have ever experienced before, or may ever experience again.

You have just taken a heroic journey through the Water Caves. Now rest for awhile. Because there is still more to experience as you continue spending priceless moments of time at Friar Park.

Ye Memories to Cherish

Ye memories to cherish upon leaving Friar Park

Today one of your dreams came true. You entered the grounds of Friar Park and visited many of its gorgeous gardens. You even saw the south & east facades of the house. Perhaps most interesting of all, you rowed through the underground water caves. It has been quite a day. There is so much more to see, but it would not be possible to see it all at one time. Especially if you want to take your time, and really appreciate all that Frank Crisp and his team created.

The night sky has descended down upon Friar Park, so it makes sense to go back to where you came from and return another time. Don't worry. Everything will still be here when you are ready to return. Friar Park is not going anywhere. Especially if you are willing to travel back in time, as you did today. But always remember that you do not have to physically visit Friar Park to learn all but it, and to be inspired by it. We have plenty of stories to tell and for you to listen to. Together, we can visit Friar Park anytime we want to, especially our favorite times, which was when it was new, and one of the most fantastic country homes in the world, between 1895 - 1919, when Frank Crisp and his family lived here.

You walk forward on the foot path along the south portion of the lake to your right and then turn left at the Stone of Precation. You now walk down the driveway and see the miniature woodland - where the California Pines grow with great pride - is on your right. The Alpine Meadow is on your left. You now walk past the path leading down to the Gloomie Glenne. The striking Scarlet Oaks are further on your left. As you continue to walk you soon pass the sign that says DON'T KEEP OFF THE GRASS and you realize that you did indeed walk upon the grass.

As you continue on, you pass the Lower Lodge. The ornate security gates mysteriously open as you approach. As you prepare to pass over the threshold on your way out you realize that you are taking a priceless treasure with you. Don't worry. No one in the lodge or at the gates will stop you from taking it with you, because you wouldn't be the only one. Everyone who leaves here has in their possession the same treasure. Friar Park has an endless supply to offer, so be sure to share it with others. Because the treasure you are taking is a collection of positive and uplifting and inspirational stories about a beautiful place, and the geniuses who created it. Such spectacular stories are worth sharing, and that is why we are sharing ours with you and anyone who wants to know more about Friar Park.

So as you pass over the threshold and the gates close behind you and you return to the normal world and your own time today - right now - you look up and see a shimmering comet as it flashes overhead in the deepest and darkest recesses of the midnight sky. What could that mean? Can Sir Frank's illusions follow you outside of these gates? Perhaps it was just a comet flying by. Or perhaps it was a sign for you to always remember that no matter if - or when - you ever went to this unique estate, with it's **"Museum of Gardens"**, and no matter whether you ever met him or not, Sir Frank Crisp hopes that you have enjoyed and appreciated the peaceful & educational and inspirational time you have spent walking along the paths, and upon the grass, and anywhere and everywhere you wanted to go on the fabulous estate known as Friar Park.

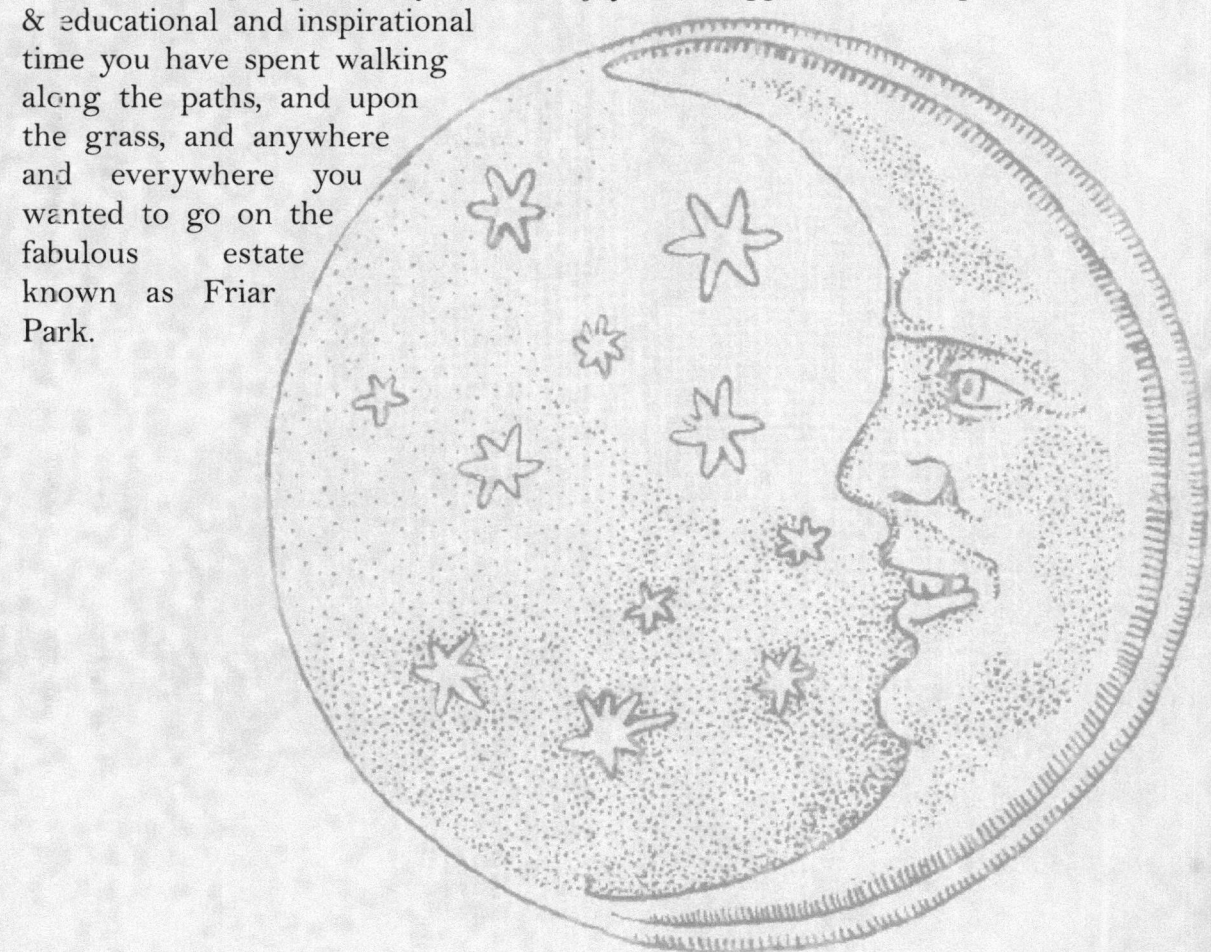

Books of Interest

Friar Park: A Pictorial History *by Scott Cardinals*

Friar Park. 1919 Estate Auction Catalogue *by Scott Cardinals*

Greetings from Friar Park (Henley-on-Thames): An archive of postcards celebrating the estate of The Beatles' George Harrison *by Scott Cardinal*

A Grand Tour of the Dakota Apartments: A Journey Through Time of the Interior & Exterior of New York's Legendary Landmark *by Scott Cardinal*

The Dakota Apartments: A Pictorial History of New York's Legendary Landmark *by Scott Cardinal*

The Dakota Scrapbook: Volume 1. Exterior *by Scott Cardinal*

Tittenhurst Park: History, Gardens, & Architecture (Volume 1) *by Scott Cardinal*

Tittenhurst Park: John Lennon & Yoko Ono (Volume 2) *by Scott Cardinal*

Tittenhurst Park: Ringo Starr & the Sheikh (Volume 3) *by Scott Cardinal*

Tittenhurst Park: A Pictorial History *by Scott Cardinal*

Tittenhurst Park: An Illustrated History *by Scott Cardinal*

Audible Adventures

Please visit **AudibleAdventures.com** and enjoy listening to professional narrators of audio walking tours of Friar Park and other places of major architectural and historical significance.

www.ingramcontent.com/pod-product-compliance
Lightning Source LLC
Chambersburg PA
CBHW042030150426
43199CB00003B/23